J   Glimpses of Louisa

GLIMPSES OF LOUISA

GLIMPSES OF LOUISA

A Centennial Sampling of the

Best Short Stories

by

LOUISA MAY ALCOTT

Selected with an Introduction and Editor's Notes by

CORNELIA MEIGS

LITTLE, BROWN AND COMPANY
Boston   Toronto

Published simultaneously in Canada
by Little, Brown & Company (Canada) Limited

PRINTED IN THE UNITED STATES OF AMERICA

INTRODUCTION

It is a question that is asked of many writers: "Where do you get your ideas?" If the answer is given directly and accurately it ought to be: "One doesn't get ideas; they come." And of all the people of whom this is true, it would be most true of Louisa Alcott.

Ideas seemed to come to her from everywhere, from the places where she went, from the people she met, from incidents that she observed or of which she heard. Her mind was always active, thinking of why people did this and that or of what would happen in beautiful or interesting places, or wondering, when she caught a glimpse of some specially noticeable person, how he or she would behave if such and such a thing happened. For her, material for stories was everywhere and she kept gathering it up, putting this and that together, remembering some fancied beginning and suddenly coming across what would make a good end.

Her longer works which brought her such fame and affection — *Little Women, An Old-Fashioned Girl, Little Men, Eight Cousins, Rose in Bloom, Jack and Jill, Under the Lilacs* and *Jo's Boys*, were all written after she was over thirty years old. Her fame came with *Little Women*, but her work as a writer began long before that. Like a great many young persons who set out to be authors, she began with short stories. It always looks as though they are easier to write than longer works, but that is not true, except for certain people. In her time the fashion was for stories to be wildly adventurous, whether they were believable or not, and about distant places of which neither reader nor writer knew very much.

She had begun, even when she was a very small child, to be interested in books, and she played with those in her father's library, pretending both to herself and to other people that she could read, and filling the blank flyleaves of the dictionary and other heavy works with scribbling, pretending also that she could write. As soon, in fact, as she learned to write legibly she began putting down stories, and once she got the idea that she might earn money by them, she unfortunately fell into the way of composing the kind of lurid tales which were in immediate demand. At this period she was getting her ideas out of books rather than from the world around her, for she thought that this was how an author should write. She was, in fact, teaching herself how to write and, in the end, how not to. There was no one to teach her; she was obliged to teach herself.

She never went to school; she was taught at home by her father. He was a deeply clever man with many new and bold ideas about children's education, but he was no writer himself. Many people have left records that as a talker he was charming and interesting, but when it came to writing his style was heavy and complex, as fitted his deep philosophy, for he was one of the important thinkers of his time. Fortunately he was not to hand on this style to his daughter; instead she began to find her own way. Her journal gives the titles of a number of her earliest stories which were published, but she never mentions them again. After she became famous as the author of *Little Women*, publishers would have been glad to go back and print anything she had written, but she did not make the mistake of taking advantage of this profitable demand. She knew that with these early stories she was merely learning to write, so she put the unskilled efforts aside. One thing of great value her father did give her: he brought her to understand and love his own favorite book, *The Pilgrim's Progress*. No one can read John Bunyan's matchless prose with its simplicity and grace and not be influenced by it. Louisa, beyond a doubt, got some of her easy flow of words from it, as well as her compact method of saying much in brief that availed her so well later.

Even after her experience with *Little Women* showed her that writing about real things with which she was familiar, and real people whom she knew and loved, was her true and proper field, she continued to write short stories; for every place she went and all the people she knew suggested them. The short stories came to be overshadowed by her longer books, but they had liveliness and vividness of their own and are well worth reexamining today. They tell so truly about actual living that we forget, many times, that they are a hundred years old, and only a chance quaint detail will bring us suddenly to remember that they were written in another age. In one story a young girl is invited to a Harvard Class Day and she declares in a great flutter that she cannot possibly go without a new dress and that it must have a train! And it is only in the midst of a tale about bicycles that one suddenly realizes that the machines the author is thinking of are the great tall kind with one huge wheel in front and a very small one behind to help with the balance. When the present-day bicycles with two wheels of equal size were invented, they were called safety bicycles or, for short, "safeties."

Another fashion of her time declared that writing, particularly for young readers, must teach a lesson, and that lesson must be thoroughly explained. Against this idea she firmly rebelled, understanding that preaching at young readers was not the best way to convince them of what they ought or ought not to do. So very insistent was this custom that even with her effort against it she occasionally falls into what we, in our more critical day, might call preaching, but it is reduced to very small proportion instead of being the most conspicuous feature of the whole tale. She developed very fully the art of giving an example of the truth she wanted to convey, rather than preaching about it. Her belief was that the great task of everyone was to learn how to live in relation

to oneself, to the people about one and to God. It comes impercep-
tibly into all her work, but a reader who has been in company with
Miss Alcott through the length of any book finds suddenly that
she has, with the reading, learned a good deal about living which
she did not know before.

It is true that the very best of what she has left us to cherish for
a hundred years lies in her longer works where she gives herself
room to show her characters, with whom the reader gets closely
and affectionately acquainted, watching them change, develop,
make their mistakes, overcome their difficulties and arrive where
they had set out to go, or rather, where Louisa had set out to take
them. In this method her gifts amount to quiet genius, for genius
is the only word which can describe that inexplicable gift for making people and their surroundings real.

Yet in spite of her realization of where her best course lay, she
continued writing short stories, leaving a very great store of them
behind her. After *Little Women*, after she became famous, collections of her stories kept coming out, but they were of her own
selection. Only one or two of the early lurid tales did she allow to
appear, in answer to the curiosity of her young readers about "Jo
March's necessity stories." "The Baron's Gloves" is one. "The
Spectre Bridegroom" is another, in which the bride is a daughter
of the high nobility, whose hand in marriage her proud father had
refused to a humble suitor. When she finally came into her own as
a famous author, Louisa was quite content to have to do with
rather less exalted classes of society.

From the year of publication of *Little Women*, 1868, the longer
books came out regularly, at first one every year, later in alternate
years, and at last at longer intervals. The last, *Jo's Boys* appeared
in 1887, the year before her death. But during this period there
was an equally long succession of short story collections: *Aunt Jo's
Scrap-Bag* in six volumes between 1872 and 1883, *Lulu's Library*
in three volumes, between 1886 and 1889, the last appearing after
Louisa herself was gone. *Lulu's Library* contained stories for

younger children, mostly fanciful and fairy stories. Lulu was Louisa Neiriker, who came to live with her aunt after the death of her mother, May (Amy). Single volume collections came during this same period: *Silver Pitchers, Proverb Stories, Spinning Wheel Stories*, and *A Garland for Girls*, this last one published in the same year as *Jo's Boys*. The stories which follow are gathered from these collections. Since Louisa put into everything she wrote so much of herself, her thoughts and feelings, we have here, for our future recollection, many new glimpses of Louisa Alcott herself.

CONTENTS

ONAWANDAH

from *Spinning Wheel Stories*, 1884

In a letter to Mary Mapes Dodge, longtime editor of the young people's magazine St. Nicholas, *Louisa Alcott said, "I like the idea of* Spinning Wheel Stories *and can do several for a series. A Christmas party of children might be at an old farmhouse and hunt up the wheel and grandma spins and tells the first story. Being snowbound, others amuse the young folks each evening with more tales with a thread running through all from the wheel that enters the first one."*

By the second century of the settlement of New England there were many towns in western Massachusetts, each of which had its own record of Indian raids. This story, as Louisa Alcott presents it, is supposedly told by "Aunt Elinor," who gives it this introduction:

"The hero is an Indian, and a brave one, as you will see. I learned the little tale from an old woman who lived in the valley of the Connecticut, which the Indians called the Long River of Pines."

ONAWANDAH

Long ago — when hostile Indians haunted the great forests, and every settlement had its fort for the protection of the inhabitants — in one of the towns on the Connecticut River lived Parson Bain and his little son and daughter. The wife and mother was dead; but an old servant took care of them, and did her best to make Reuben and Eunice good children. Her direct threat, when they were naughty, was, "The Indians will come and fetch you, if you don't behave." So they grew up in great fear of the red men. Even the friendly Indians, who sometimes came for food or powder, were regarded with suspicion by the people. No man went to work without his gun nearby. On Sundays, when they trudged to the rude meeting-house, all carried the trusty rifle on the shoulder; and while the pastor preached, a sentinel mounted guard at the door, to give warning if canoes came down the river or a dark face peered from the wood.

One autumn night, when the first heavy rains were falling and a cold wind whistled through the valley, a knock came at the minister's door, and, opening it, he found an Indian boy, ragged, hungry, and footsore, who begged for food and shelter. In his broken way, he told how he had fallen ill, and been left to die by enemies who had taken him from his own people, months before; how he had wandered for days till almost sinking; and that he had come now to ask for help, led by the hospitable light in the parsonage window.

"Send him away, master, or harm will come of it. He is a spy, and we shall all be scalped by the murdering Injuns who are wait-ing in the wood," said old Becky, harshly; while little Eunice hid in the old servant's ample skirts, and twelve-year-old Reuben laid his hand on his crossbow, ready to defend his sister if need be.

But the good man drew the poor lad in, saying, with his friendly smile: "Shall not a Christian be as hospitable as a godless savage? Come in, child, and be fed; you sorely need rest and shelter."

Leaving his face to express the gratitude he had no words to tell, the boy sat by the comfortable fire and ate like a famished wolf, while Becky muttered her forebodings and the children eyed the dark youth at a safe distance. Something in his pinched face, wounded foot, and eyes full of dumb pain and patience, touched the little girl's tender heart, and, yielding to a pitiful impulse, she brought her own basin of new milk and, setting it beside the stran-ger, ran to hide behind her father, suddenly remembering that this was one of the dreaded Indians.

"That was well done, little daughter. Thou shalt love thine ene-mies, and share thy bread with the needy. See, he is smiling; that pleased him, and he wishes us to be his friends."

But Eunice ventured no more that night, and quaked in her little bed at the thought of the strange boy sleeping on a blanket before the fire below. Reuben hid his fears better, and resolved to watch while others slept; but was off as soon as his curly head touched the pillow, and dreamed of tomahawks and war-whoops till morning.

Next day, neighbors came to see the waif, and one and all ad-vised sending him away as soon as possible, since he was doubt-less a spy, as Becky said, and would bring trouble of some sort.

"When he is well, he may go whithersoever he will; but while he is too lame to walk, weak with hunger, and worn out with wear-iness, I will harbor him. He cannot feign suffering and starvation like this. I shall do my duty and leave the consequences to the

Lord," answered the parson, with such pious firmness that the neighbors said no more.

But they kept a close watch upon Onawandah, when he went among them, silent and submissive, but with the proud air of a captive prince, and sometimes a fierce flash in his black eyes when the other lads taunted him with his red skin. He was very lame for weeks, and could only sit in the sun, weaving pretty baskets for Eunice, and shaping bows and arrows for Reuben. The children were soon his friends, for with them he was always gentle, trying in his soft language and expressive gestures to show his goodwill and gratitude; for they defended him against their ruder play-mates, and, following their father's example, trusted and cherished the homeless youth.

When he was able to walk, he taught the boy to shoot and trap the wild creatures of the wood, to find fish where others failed, and to guide himself in the wilderness by star and sun, wind and water. To Eunice he brought little offerings of bark and feathers; taught her to make moccasins of skin, belts of shells, or pouches gay with porcupine quills and colored grass. He would not work for old Becky — who plainly showed her distrust — saying: "A brave does not grind corn and bring wood; that is squaw's work. Onawandah will hunt and fish and fight for you, but no more." And even the request of the parson could not win obedience in this, though the boy would have died for the good man.

"We cannot tame an eagle as we can a barnyard fowl. Let him remember only kindness of us, and so we turn a foe into a friend," said Parson Bain, stroking the sleek, dark head that always bowed before him with a docile reverence shown to no other living creature.

Winter came, and the settlers fared hardly through the long months, when the drifts rose to the eaves of their low cabins, and the stores, carefully harvested, failed to supply even their simple wants. But the minister's family never lacked wild meat, for Onawandah proved himself a better hunter than any man in the town; and the boy of sixteen led the way on his snowshoes when they went to track a bear to its den, chase the deer for miles, or shoot the wolves that howled about their homes in the winter nights.

But he never joined in their games, and sat apart when the young folk made merry, as if he scorned such childish pastimes and longed to be a man in all things. Why he stayed when he was well again, no one could tell, unless he waited for spring to make his way to his own people. But Reuben and Eunice rejoiced to keep him; for while he taught them many things, he was their pupil also, learning English rapidly, and proving himself a very affectionate and devoted friend and servant, in his own quiet way.

"Be of good cheer, little daughter; I shall be gone but three days, and our brave Onawandah will guard you well," said the parson one April morning, as he mounted his horse to visit a distant settlement, where the bitter winter had brought sickness and death to more than one household.

The boy showed his white teeth in a bright smile as he stood beside the children, while Becky croaked, with a shake of the head:

"I hope you mayn't find you've warmed a viper in your bosom, master."

Two days later it seemed as if Becky was a true prophet, and that the confiding minister *had* been terribly deceived; for Onawandah went away to hunt, and that night the awful war-whoop woke the sleeping villagers, to find their houses burning, while the hidden Indians shot at them by the light of the fires kindled by dusky scouts. In terror and confusion the whites flew to the fort; and while the men fought bravely, the women held blankets to catch arrows and bullets, or bound up the hurts of their defenders.

It was all over by daylight, and the red men sped away up the river with several prisoners and such booty as they could plunder from the deserted houses. Not till all fear of a return of their enemies was over did the poor people venture to leave the fort and seek their ruined homes. Then it was discovered that Becky and the parson's children were gone, and great was the bewailing, for the good man was much beloved by all his flock.

Suddenly the smothered voice of Becky was heard by a party of visitors, calling dolefully:

"I am here, betwixt the beds. Pull me out, neighbors, for I am half dead with fright and smothering."

The old woman was quickly extricated from her hiding place, and with much energy declared that she had seen Onawandah, disguised with war-paint, among the Indians, and that he had torn away the children from her arms before she could fly from the house.

"He chose his time well, when they were defenseless, dear lambs! Spite of all my warnings, master trusted him, and this is the thanks we get. Oh, my poor master! How can I tell him this heavy news?"

There was no need to tell it; for as Becky sat moaning and beating her breast on the fireless hearth, and the sympathizing neighbors stood about her, the sound of a horse's hoofs was heard, and the parson came down the hilly road like one riding for his life. He had seen the smoke afar off, guessed the sad truth, and hurried on, to find his home in ruins, and to learn by his first glance at the faces around him that his children were gone.

When he had heard all there was to tell, he sat down upon his door-stone with his head in his hands, praying for strength to bear a grief too deep for words. The wounded and weary men tried to comfort him with hope, and the women wept with him as they hugged their own babies closer to the hearts that ached for the lost children. Suddenly a stir went through the mournful group, as Onawandah came from the wood with a young deer upon his shoulders, and amazement in his face as he saw the desolation before him. Dropping his burden, he stood an instant looking with eyes that kindled fiercely; then he came bounding toward them, undaunted by the hatred, suspicion, and surprise plainly written on the countenances before him. He missed his playmates, and asked but one question:

"The boy, the little squaw — where gone?"

His answer was a rough one, for the men seized him and poured forth the tale, heaping reproaches upon him for such treachery and ingratitude. He bore it all in proud silence till they pointed to the poor father, whose dumb sorrow was more eloquent than all their wrath. Onawandah looked at him, and the fire died out of his eyes as if quenched by the tears he would not shed. Shaking off the hands that held him, he went to his good friend, saying with passionate earnestness:

"Onawandah is *not* traitor! Onawandah remembers! Onawandah grateful! You believe?"

The poor parson looked up at him, and could not doubt his truth; for genuine love and sorrow ennobled the dark face, and he had never known the boy to lie.

"I believe and trust you still, but others will not. Go, you are no longer safe here, and I have no home to offer you," said the parson sadly, feeling that he cared for none unless his children were restored to him.

"Onawandah has no fear. He goes; but he comes again to bring the boy, the little squaw."

Few words, but they were so solemnly spoken that the most unbelieving were impressed; for the youth laid one hand on the gray head bowed before him, and lifted the other toward heaven, as if calling the Great Spirit to hear his vow.

A relenting murmur went through the crowd, but the boy paid no heed as he turned away, and with no arms but his hunting knife and bow, no food but such as he could find, no guide but the sun by day, the stars by night, plunged into the pathless forest and was gone.

Then the people drew a long breath, and muttered to one another: "He will never do it, yet he is a brave lad for his years."

"Only a shift to get off with a whole skin, I warrant you. These varlets are as cunning as foxes," added Becky, sourly.

The parson alone believed and hoped, though weeks and months went by and his children did not come.

Meantime, Reuben and Eunice were far away in an Indian camp, resting as best they could, after the long journey that followed that dreadful night. Their captors were not cruel to them, for Reuben was a stout fellow, and thanks to Onawandah could hold his own with the boys who would have tormented him if he had been feeble or cowardly. Eunice also was a hardy creature for her years, and when her first fright and fatigue were over, made herself useful in many ways among the squaws, who did not let the pretty child suffer greatly, though she was neglected because they knew no better.

Life in a wigwam was not a life of ease, and fortunately the children were accustomed to simple habits and the hardships that all endured in those early times. But they mourned for home till their young faces were pathetic with the longing, and their pillows of dry leaves were often wet with tears in the night. Their clothes grew ragged, their hair unkempt, their faces tanned by sun and wind. Scanty food and exposure to all weathers tried the strength of their bodies, and uncertainty as to their fate saddened their spirits; yet they bore up bravely, and said their prayers faithfully, feeling sure that God would bring them home to father in His own good time.

One day, when Reuben was snaring birds in the wood — for the Indians had no fear of such young children venturing to escape — he heard the cry of a quail, and followed it deeper and deeper into the forest, till it ceased, and with a sudden rustle Onawandah rose up from the brakes, his finger on his lips to prevent any exclamation that might betray him to other ears and eyes.

"I come for you and little Laroka" (the name he gave Eunice, meaning "Wild Rose"). "I take you home. Not know me yet. Go and wait."

He spoke low and fast; but the joy in his face told how glad he was to find the boy after his long search, and Reuben clung to him, trying not to disgrace himself by crying like a girl in his surprise and delight.

Lying hidden in the tall brakes they talked in whispers, while one told of the capture, and the other of a plan of escape; for, though a friendly tribe, these Indians were not Onawandah's people, and they must not suspect that he knew the children, else they might be separated at once.

"Little squaw betray me. You watch her. Tell her not to cry out, not speak me any time. When I say come, we go — fast — in the night. Not ready yet."

These were the orders Reuben received, and when he could compose himself he went back to the wigwams, leaving his friend in the wood, while he told the good news to Eunice and prepared her for the part she must play.

Fear had taught her self-control, and the poor child stood the test well, working off her relief and rapture by pounding corn on the stone mortar till her little hands were blistered, and her arms ached for hours afterward.

Not till the next day did Onawandah make his appearance, and then he came limping into the village, weary, lame, and half starved, after his long wandering in the wilderness. He was kindly welcomed, and his story believed; for he told only the first part, and said nothing of his life among the white men. He hardly glanced at the children when they were pointed out to him by their captors, and scowled at poor Eunice, who forgot her part in her joy and smiled as she met the dark eyes that till now had always looked kindly at her. A touch from Reuben warned her, and she was glad to hide her confusion by shaking her long hair over her face, as if afraid of the stranger.

Onawandah took no further notice of them, but seemed to be very lame with the old wound in his foot, which prevented his being obliged to hunt with the men. He was resting and slowly gathering strength for the hard task he had set himself, while he waited for a safe time to save the children. They understood, but the suspense proved too much for little Eunice, and she pined with impatience to be gone. She lost appetite and color, and cast such appealing glances at Onawandah that he could not seem quite indifferent, and gave her a soft word now and then, or did such acts of kindness as he could perform unsuspected. When she lay awake at night thinking of home, a cricket would chirp outside the wigwam, and a hand slip in a leaf full of berries, or a bark-cup of fresh water for the feverish little mouth. Sometimes it was only a caress or a whisper of encouragement that reassured the childish heart and sent her to sleep with a comfortable sense of love and protection, like a sheltering wing over a motherless bird.

Reuben stood it better, and entered heartily into the excitement of the plot; for he had grown tall and strong in these trying months, and felt that he must prove himself a man to sustain and defend his sister. Quietly he put away each day a bit of dried meat, a handful of parched corn, or a well-sharpened arrowhead, as provision for the journey; while Onawandah seemed to be amusing himself with making moccasins and a little vest of deerskin for an Indian child about the age of Eunice.

At last, in the early autumn, all the men went off on the war-path, leaving only boys and women behind. Then Onawandah's eyes began to kindle, and Reuben's heart to beat fast, for both felt that their time for escape had come.

All was ready, and one moonless night the signal was given. A cricket chirped shrilly outside the tent where the children slept with one old squaw. A strong hand cut the skin beside their bed of fir boughs, and two trembling creatures crept out to follow the tall shadow that flitted noiselessly before them into the darkness of the wood. Not a broken twig, a careless step, or a whispered word betrayed them, and they vanished as swiftly and silently as hunted deer flying for their lives.

Till dawn they hurried on, Onawandah carrying Eunice, whose strength soon failed, and Reuben manfully shouldering the hatchet and the pouch of food. At sunrise they hid in a thicket by a spring and rested, while waiting for the friendly night to come again. Then they pushed on, and fear gave wings to their feet, so that by another morning they were far enough away to venture to travel more slowly and sleep at night.

If the children had learned to love and trust the Indian boy in happier times, they adored him now, and came to regard him as an earthly Providence; so faithful, brave, and tender was he — so forgetful of himself, so bent on saving them. He never seemed to sleep, ate the poorest morsels, or went without any food when provision failed; let no danger daunt him, no hardship wring complaint from him, but went on through the wild forest, led by guides invisible to them, till they began to hope that home was near.

Twice he saved their lives. Once when he went in search of food, leaving Reuben to guard his sister, the children, being very hungry, ignorantly ate some poisonous berries which looked like wild cherries and were deliciously sweet. The boy generously gave most of them to Eunice, and soon was terror-stricken to see her grow pale, and cold, and deathly ill. Not knowing what to do, he could only rub her hands and call wildly for Onawandah.

The name echoed through the silent wood, and though far away, the keen ear of the Indian heard it, his fleet feet brought him back in time, and his knowledge of wild roots and herbs made it possible to save the child when no other help was at hand.

"Make fire. Keep warm. I soon come," he said, after hearing the story and examining Eunice, who could only lift her eyes to him, full of childish confidence and patience.

Then he was off again, scouring the woods like a hound on the scent, searching everywhere for the precious little herb that would counteract the poison. Anyone watching him would have thought him crazy, as he rushed hither and thither, tearing up the leaves, creeping on his hands and knees that it might not escape him, and when he found it, springing up with a cry that startled the birds and carried hope to poor Reuben, who was trying to forget his own pain in his anxiety for Eunice, whom he thought dying.

"Eat, eat, while I make drink. All safe now," cried Onawandah, as he came leaping toward them with his hands full of green leaves and his dark face shining with joy.

The boy was soon relieved, but for hours they hung over the girl, who suffered sadly, till she grew unconscious and lay as if dead. Reuben's courage failed then, and he cried bitterly, thinking how hard it would be to leave the dear little creature under the pines and go home alone to father. Even Onawandah lost hope for a while, and sat like a bronze statue of despair, with his eyes fixed on his Wild Rose, who seemed fading away too soon.

Suddenly he rose, stretched his arms to the west, where the sun was setting splendidly, and in his own musical language prayed to the Great Spirit. The Christian boy fell upon his knees, feeling that the only help was in the Father who saw and heard them even in the wilderness. Both were comforted, and when they turned to Eunice there was a faint tinge of color on the pale cheeks, as if the evening red kissed her; the look of pain was gone, and she slept quietly, without the moans that had made their hearts ache before.

"He hears! He hears!" cried Onawandah, and for the first time Reuben saw tears in his keen eyes, as the Indian boy turned his face to the sky, full of a gratitude that no words were sweet enough to tell.

All night Eunice lay peacefully sleeping, and the moon lighted Onawandah's lonely watch, for Reuben was worn out with suspense and slept beside his sister.

In the morning she was safe, and great was the rejoicing; but for two days the little invalid was not allowed to continue the journey, much as they longed to hurry on. It was a pretty sight, the bed of hemlock boughs spread under a green tent of woven branches, and on the pillow of moss the pale child watching the flicker of sunshine through the leaves, listening to the babble of a brook close by, or sleeping tranquilly, lulled by the murmur of the pines. Patient, loving, and grateful, it was a pleasure to serve her, and both the lads were faithful nurses. Onawandah cooked birds for her to eat, and made a pleasant drink of the wild raspberry leaves to quench her thirst. Reuben snared rabbits, that she might have nourishing food, and longed to shoot a deer for provision, that she might not suffer hunger again on their journey. This boy-ish desire led him deeper into the wood than it was wise for him to go alone, for it was near nightfall, and wild creatures haunted the forest in those days. The fire, which Onawandah kept constantly burning, guarded their little camp where Eunice lay; but Reuben, with no weapon but his bow and hunting knife, was beyond this protection when he at last gave up his vain hunt and turned home-ward. Suddenly, the sound of stealthy steps startled him, but he could see nothing through the dusk at first, and hurried on, fear-ing that some treacherous Indian was following him. Then he re-membered his sister and resolved not to betray her resting-place if he could help it, for he had learned courage of Onawandah, and longed to be as brave and generous as his dusky hero.

So he paused to watch and wait, and soon saw the gleam of two fiery eyes, not behind, but above him, in a tree. Then he knew that it was an "Indian devil," as they called a species of fierce animal that lurked in the thickets and sprang on its prey like a small tiger.

"If I could only kill it alone, how proud Onawandah would be of me," thought Reuben, burning for the good opinion of his friend.

It would have been wiser to hurry on and give the beast no time to spring; but the boy was over-bold, and fitting an arrow to the string, aimed at the bright eyeball and let fly. A sharp snarl showed that some harm was done, and, rather daunted by the sav-age sound, Reuben raced away, meaning to come back next day for the prize he hoped he had secured.

But soon he heard the creature bounding after him, and he uttered one ringing shout for help, feeling too late that he had been foolhardy. Fortunately, he was nearer camp than he thought. Onawandah heard him, and was there in time to receive the beast as, mad with the pain of the wound, it sprang at Reuben. There was no time for words, and the boy could only watch in breathless interest and anxiety the fight which went on between the brute and the Indian.

It was sharp but short; for Onawandah had his knife, and as soon as he could get the snarling, struggling creature down, he killed it with a skillful stroke. But not before it had torn and bitten him more dangerously than he knew; for the dusk hid the wounds, and excitement kept him from feeling them at first. Reuben thanked him heartily, and accepted his few words of warning with grateful docility; then both hurried back to Eunice, who till next day knew nothing of her brother's danger.

Onawandah made light of his scratches, as he called them, got their supper, and sent Reuben early to bed, for tomorrow they were to start again.

Excited by his adventure, the boy slept lightly, and waking in the night saw by the flicker of the fire Onawandah binding up a deep wound in his breast with wet moss and his own belt. A stifled groan betrayed how much he suffered; but when Reuben went to him he would accept no help, said it was nothing, and sent him back to bed, preferring to endure the pain in stern silence, with true Indian pride and courage.

Next morning, they set out and pushed on as fast as Eunice's strength allowed. But it was evident that Onawandah suffered much, though he would not rest, forbade the children to speak of his wounds, and pressed on with feverish haste, as if he feared that his strength might not hold out. Reuben watched him anxiously, for there was a look in his face that troubled the boy and filled him with alarm, as well as with remorse and love. Eunice would not let him carry her as before, but trudged bravely behind him, though her feet ached and her breath often failed as she tried to keep up; and both children did all they could to comfort and sustain their friend, who seemed glad to give his life for them.

In three days they reached the river, and as if Heaven helped them in their greatest need found a canoe, left by some hunter near the shore. In they sprang, and let the swift current bear them along, Eunice kneeling in the bow like a little figurehead of Hope, Reuben steering with his paddle, and Onawandah sitting with arms tightly folded over his breast, as if to control the sharp anguish of the neglected wound. He knew that it was past help now, and only cared to see the children safe; then, worn out but happy, he was proud to die, having paid his debt to the good parson, and proved that he was not a liar nor a traitor.

Hour after hour they floated down the great river, looking eagerly for signs of home, and when at last they entered the familiar valley, while the little girl cried for joy, and the boy paddled as he had never done before, Onawandah sat erect, with his haggard eyes fixed on the dim distance, and sang his death-song in a clear, strong voice — though every breath was pain — bent on dying like a brave, without complaint or fear.

At last they saw the smoke from the cabins on the hillside, and hastily mooring the canoe, all sprang out, eager to be at home after their long and perilous wandering. But as his foot touched the land, Onawandah felt that he could do no more, and stretching his arms toward the parsonage, the windows of which glimmered as hospitably as they had done when he first saw them, he said, with a pathetic sort of triumph in his broken voice: "Go. I cannot. Tell the good father Onawandah not lie, not forget. He keep his promise."

Then he dropped upon the grass and lay as if dead, while Reuben, bidding Eunice keep watch, ran as fast as his tired legs could carry him to tell the tale and bring help.

The little girl did her part tenderly, carrying water in her hands to wet the white lips, tearing up her ragged skirt to lay fresh bandages on the wound that had been bleeding the brave boy's life away, and, sitting by him, gathered his head into her arms, begging him to wait till father came.

But poor Onawandah had waited too long; now he could only look up into the dear, loving little face bent over him, and whisper wistfully: "Wild Rose will remember Onawandah?" as the light went out of his eyes, and his last breath was a smile for her.

When the parson and his people came hurrying up full of wonder, joy, and goodwill, they found Eunice weeping bitterly, and the Indian boy lying like a young warrior smiling at death.

"Ah, my neighbors, the savage has taught us a lesson we never can forget. Let us imitate his virtues and do honor to his memory," said the pastor, as he held his little daughter close and looked down at the pathetic figure at his feet, whose silence was more eloquent than any words.

All felt it, and even old Becky had a remorseful sigh for the boy who had kept his word so well and given back her darlings safe.

They buried him where he lay; and for years the lonely mound under the great oak was kept green by loving hands. Wild roses bloomed there, and the murmur of the Long River of Pines was a fit lullaby for faithful Onawandah.

AN IVY SPRAY AND
LADIES' SLIPPERS

from *A Garland for Girls*, 1886

During her last years, Miss Alcott was beset from all sides by requests from book publishers and magazine editors for stories. What she considered the most important of all were the letters from her young readers who, having read Little Women, *were constantly demanding "more of the same." Early in 1886 she wrote to her publisher, Thomas Niles, who had asked her for a novel, that she could not give him one but, "I can give you a girls' book, however, and I think that would be better than a novel." What she was offering was a series of short stories to be published together under the title of* A Garland for Girls, *"to make a companion volume for* Spinning Wheel Stories, *at Christmas if you want it."*

AN IVY SPRAY AND
LADIES' SLIPPERS

"It can't be done! So I may as well give it up and get a new pair. I long for them, but I'm afraid my nice little plan for Laura will be spoilt," said Jessie Delano to herself, as she shook her head over a pair of small, dilapidated slippers almost past mending. While she vainly pricked her fingers over them for the last time, her mind was full of girlish hopes and fears, as well as of anxieties far too serious for a lighthearted creature of sixteen.

A year ago the sisters had been the petted daughters of a rich man; but death and misfortune came suddenly, and now they were left to face poverty alone. They had few relations, and had offended the rich uncle who offered Jessie a home, because she refused to be separated from her sister. Poor Laura was an invalid, and no one wanted her; but Jessie would not leave her, so they clung together and lived on in the humble rooms where their father died, trying to earn their bread by the only accomplishments they possessed. Laura painted well, and after many disappointments was beginning to find a sale for her dainty designs and delicate flowers. Jessie had a natural gift for dancing; and her former teacher, a kindhearted Frenchwoman, offered her favorite pupil the post of assistant teacher in her classes for children.

It cost the girl a struggle to accept a place of this sort and be a humble teacher, patiently twirling stupid little boys and girls round and round over the smooth floor where she used to dance so happily when she was the pride of the class and the queen of the closing balls. But for Laura's sake she gratefully accepted the offer, glad to add her mite to their small store, and to feel that she could help keep the wolf from the door. They had seemed to hear the howl of this dreaded phantom more than once during that year, and looked forward to the long hard winter with an anxiety which neither would confess to the other. Laura feared to fall ill if she worked too hard, and then what would become of this pretty young sister who loved her so tenderly and would not be tempted to leave her? And Jessie could do very little except rebel against their hard fate and make impracticable plans. But each worked bravely, talked cheerfully, and waited hopefully for some good fortune to befall them, while doubt and pain and poverty and care made the young hearts so heavy that the poor girls often fell asleep on pillows wet with secret tears.

The smaller trials of life beset Jessie at this particular moment, and her bright wits were trying to solve the problem of how to spend her treasured five dollars on slippers for herself and paints for Laura. Both were much needed, and she had gone in shabby shoes to save up money for the little surprise on which she had set her heart; but now dismay fell upon her when the holes refused to be cobbled, and the largest of bows would not hide the worn-out toes in spite of ink and blacking lavishly applied.

"These are the last of my dear French slippers, and I can't afford any more. I hate cheap things! But I shall have to get them; for my boots are shabby, and everyone has to look at my feet when I lead. Oh dear, what a horrid thing it is to be poor!" and Jessie surveyed the shabby little shoes affectionately, as her eyes filled with tears; for the road looked very rough and steep now, when she remembered how she used to dance through life as happy as a butterfly in a garden full of sunshine and flowers.

"Now, Jess, no nonsense, no red eyes to tell tales! Go and do your errands, and come in as gay as a lark, or Laura will be worried." And springing up, the girl began to sing instead of sob, as she stirred about her dismal little room, cleaning her old gloves, mending her one white dress, and wishing with a sigh of intense longing that she could afford some flowers to wear, every ornament having been sold long ago. Then, with a kiss and a smile to her patient sister, she hurried away to get the necessary slippers and the much-desired paints, which Laura would not ask for, though her work waited for want of them.

Having been reared in luxury, poor little Jessie's tastes were all of the daintiest sort; and her hardest trial, after Laura's feeble health, was the daily sacrifice of the many comforts and elegances to which she had been accustomed. Faded gowns, cleaned gloves, and mended boots cost her many a pang, and the constant temptation of seeing pretty, useful, and unattainable things was a very hard one. Laura rarely went out, and so was spared this cross; then she was three years older, had always been delicate, and lived much in a happy world of her own. So Jessie bore her trials silently, but sometimes felt very covetous and resentful to see so much pleasure, money, and beauty in the world, and yet have so little of it fall to her lot.

"I feel as if I could pick a pocket today and not mind a bit, if it were a rich person's. It's a shame, when papa was always so generous, that no one remembers us. If ever I'm rich again, I'll just hunt up all the poor girls I can find, and give them nice shoes, if nothing else," she thought, as she went along the crowded streets, pausing involuntarily at the shop windows to look with longing eyes at the treasures within.

Resisting the allurements of French slippers with bows and buckles, she wisely bought a plain, serviceable pair, and trudged away, finding balm for her wounds in the fact that they were very cheap. More balm came when she met a young friend, who joined her as she stood wistfully eyeing the piles of grapes in a window and longing to buy some for Laura.

This warmhearted schoolmate read the wish before Jessie saw her, and gratified it so adroitly that the girl could accept the pretty basketful sent to her sister without feeling like a spendthrift or a beggar. It comforted her very much, and the world began to look brighter after that little touch of kindness, as it always does when genuine sympathy makes sunshine in shady places.

At the art store she was told that more of Laura's autumn flowers were in demand; and her face was so full of innocent delight and gratitude it quite touched the old man who sold her the paints, and gave her more than her money's worth, remembering his own hard times and pitying the pretty young girl whose father he had known.

So Jessie did not have to pretend very hard at being "as gay as a lark" when she got home and showed her treasures. Laura was so happy over the unexpected gifts that the dinner of bread and milk and grapes was quite a picnic; and Jessie found a smile on her face when she went to dress for her party.

It was only a child's party at the house of one of Mademoiselle's pupils, and Jessie was merely invited to help the little people through their dancing. She did not like to go in this way, as she was sure to meet familiar faces there, full of the pity, curiosity, or indifference so hard for a girl to bear. But Mademoiselle asked it as a favor, and Jessie was grateful; so she went, expecting no pleasure and certain of much weariness, if not annoyance.

When she was ready — and it did not take long to slip on the white woollen dress, brush out the curly dark hair, and fold up slippers and gloves — she stood before her glass looking at herself, quite conscious that she was very pretty, with her large eyes, blooming cheeks, and the lofty little air which nothing could change. She was also painfully conscious that her dress was neither fresh nor becoming without a bit of ribbon or a knot of flowers to give it the touch of color it needed. She had an artistic eye, and used to delight in ordering charming costumes for herself in the happy days when all her wishes were granted as if fairies still lived. She tossed over her very small store of ribbons in vain; everything had been worn till neither beauty nor freshness remained.

"Oh dear! where *can* I find something to make me look less like a nun — and a very shabby one, too?" she said, longing for the pink corals she sold to pay Laura's doctor's bill.

The sound of a soft tap, tap, tap, startled her, and she ran to open the door. No one was there but Laura, fast asleep on the sofa. Tap, tap, tap! went the invisible hand; and as the sound seemed to come from the window, Jessie glanced that way, thinking her tame dove had come to be fed. Neither hungry dove nor bold sparrow appeared — only a spray of Japanese ivy waving in the wind. A very pretty spray it was, covered with tiny crimson leaves; and it tapped impatiently, as if it answered her question by saying, "Here is a garland for you; come and take it."

Jessie's quick eye was caught at once by the fine color, and running to the window she looked out as eagerly as if a new idea had come into her head. It was a dull November day, and the prospect of sheds, ash barrels, and old brooms was a gloomy one; but the whole of the house glowed with the red tendrils of the hardy vine that clung to and covered the dingy bricks with a royal mantle, as if eager to cheer the eyes and hearts of all who looked. It preached a little sermon of courage, aspiration, and content to those who had the skill to read it, and bade them see how, springing from the scanty soil of that back yard full of the commonest objects, the humblest work, it set its little creepers in the crannies of the stone, and struggled up to find the sun and air, till it grew strong and beautiful — making the blank wall green in summer, glorious in autumn, and a refuge in winter, when it welcomed the sparrows to the shelter of its branches where the sun lay warmest.

Jessie loved this beautiful neighbor, and had enjoyed it all that summer — the first she ever spent in the hot city. She felt the grace its greenness gave to all it touched, and half unconsciously imitated it in trying to be brave and bright, as she also climbed up from the dismal place where she seemed shut away from everything lovely, till she was beginning to discover that the blue sky was over all, the sun still shone for her, and heaven's fresh air kissed her cheeks as kindly as ever. Many a night she had leaned from the high window when Laura was asleep, dreaming innocent dreams, living over her short past, or trying to look into the future bravely and trustfully. The little vine had felt warmer drops than rain or dew fall on it when things went badly, had heard whispered prayers when the lonely child asked the Father of the fatherless for help and comfort, had peeped in to see her sleeping peacefully when the hard hour was over, and been the first to greet her with a tap on the windowpane as she woke full of new hope in the morning. It seemed to know all her moods and troubles, to be her friend and confidante, and now came with help like a fairy godmother when our Cinderella wanted to be fine for the little ball.

"Just the thing! Why didn't I think of it? So bright and delicate and becoming? It will last better than flowers; and no one can think I'm extravagant, since it costs nothing."

As she spoke, Jessie was gathering long sprays of the rosy vine, with its glossy leaves so beautifully shaded that it was evident Jack Frost had done his best for it. Going to her glass, she fastened a wreath of the smallest leaves about her head, set a cluster of larger ones in her bosom, and then surveyed herself with girlish pleasure, as well she might; for the effect of the simple decoration was charming. Quite satisfied now, she tied on her cloud and slipped away without waking Laura, little dreaming what good fortune the ivy spray was to bring them both.

She found the children prancing with impatience to begin their ballet, much excited by the music, gaslight, and gay dresses, which made it seem like "a truly ball." All welcomed Jessie, and she soon forgot the cheap slippers, mended gloves, and old dress, as she gayly led her troop through the pretty dance with so much grace and skill that the admiring mammas who lined the walls declared it was the sweetest thing they ever saw.

"Who is that little person?" asked one of the few gentlemen who hovered about the doorways.

His hostess told Jessie's story in a few words, and was surprised to hear him say in a satisfied tone:

"I'm glad she is poor. I want her head, and now there is some chance of getting it."

"My dear Mr. Vane, what *do* you mean?" asked the lady, laughing.

"I came to study young faces; I want one for a picture, and that little girl with the red leaves is charming. Please present me."

"No use; you may ask for her hand by and by, if you like, but not for her head. She is very proud, and never would consent to sit as a model, I'm sure."

"I think I can manage it, if you will kindly give me a start."

"Very well. The children are just going down to supper, and Miss Delano will rest. You can make your bold proposal now, if you dare."

A moment later, as she stood watching the little ones troop away, Jessie found herself bowing to the tall gentleman, who begged to know what he could bring her with as much interest as if she had been the finest lady in the room. Of course she chose ice cream, and slipped into a corner to rest her tired feet, preferring the deserted parlor to the noisy dining room — not being quite sure where she belonged now.

Mr. Vane brought her a salver full of the dainties girls best love, and drawing up a table began to eat and talk in such a simple, comfortable way that Jessie could not feel shy, but was soon quite at her ease. She knew that he was a famous artist, and longed to tell him about poor Laura, who admired his pictures so much and would have enjoyed every moment of this chance interview. He was not a very young man, nor a handsome one, but he had a genial face, and the friendly manners which are so charming; and in ten minutes Jessie was chatting freely, quite unconscious that the artist was studying her in a mirror all the while. They naturally talked of the children, and after praising the pretty dance Mr. Vane quietly added:

"I've been trying to find a face among them for a picture I'm doing; but the little dears are all too young, and I must look elsewhere for a model for my wood nymph."

"Are models hard to find?" asked Jessie, eating her ice with the relish of a girl who does not often taste it.

"What I want is very hard to find. I can get plenty of beggar-girls, but this must be a refined face, young and blooming, but with poetry in it; and that does not come without a different training from any my usual models get. It will be difficult to suit me, for I'm in a hurry and don't know where to look," — which last sentence was not quite true, for the long glass showed him exactly what he wanted.

"I help Mademoiselle with her classes, and she has pupils of all ages; perhaps you could find someone there."

Jessie looked so interested that the artist felt that he had begun well, and ventured a step further as he passed the cake basket for the third time.

"You are very kind; but the trouble there is, that I fear none of the young ladies would consent to sit to me if I dared to ask them. I will confide to you that I *have* seen a head which quite suits me; but I fear I cannot get it. Give me your advice, please. Should you think this pretty creature would be offended, if I made the request most respectfully?"

"No, indeed; I should think she would be proud to help with one of your pictures, sir. My sister thinks they are very lovely; and we kept one of them when we had to sell all the rest," said Jessie in her eager, frank way.

"That was a beautiful compliment, and I am proud of it. Please tell her so, with my thanks. Which was it?"

"The woman's head — the sad, sweet one people call a Madonna. We call it Mother, and love it very much, for Laura says it is like our mother. I never saw her, but my sister remembers the dear face very well."

Jessie's eyes dropped, as if tears were near; and Mr. Vane said, in a voice which showed he understood and shared her feeling:

"I am very glad that anything of mine has been a comfort to you. I thought of my own mother when I painted that picture years ago; so you see you read it truly, and gave it the right name. Now, about the other head; you think I may venture to propose the idea to its owner, do you?"

"Why not, sir? She would be very silly to refuse, I think."

"Then *you* wouldn't be offended if asked to sit in this way?"

"Oh, no. I've sat for Laura many a time, and she says I make a very good model. But then, she only paints simple little things that I am fit for."

"That is just what I want to do. Would you mind asking the young lady for me? She is just behind you."

Jessie turned with a start, wondering who had come in; but all she saw was her own curious face in the mirror, and Mr. Vane's smiling one above it.

"Do you mean me?" she cried, so surprised and pleased and half ashamed that she could only blush and laugh and look prettier than ever.

"Indeed I do. Mrs. Murray thought the request would annoy you; but I fancied you would grant it, you wore such a graceful little garland, and seemed so interested in the pictures here."

"It is only a bit of ivy, but so pretty I wanted to wear it, as I had nothing else," said the girl, glad that her simple ornament found favor in such eyes.

"It is most artistic, and caught my eye at once. I said to myself, 'That is the head I want, and I *must* secure it if possible.' Can I?" asked Mr. Vane, smiling persuasively as he saw what a frank and artless young person he had to deal with.

"With pleasure, if Laura doesn't mind. I'll ask her, and if she is willing I shall be very proud to have even my wreath in a famous picture," answered Jessie, so full of innocent delight at being thus honored that it was a pretty sight to see.

"A thousand thanks! Now I can exult over Mrs. Murray, and

get my palette ready. When can we begin? As your sister is an invalid and cannot come to my studio with you, perhaps you will allow me to make my sketch at your own house," said Mr. Vane, as pleased with his success as only a perplexed artist could be.

"Did Mrs. Murray tell you about us?" asked Jessie quickly, as her smiles faded away and the proud look came into her face; for she was sure their misfortunes were known, since he spoke of poor Laura's health.

"A little," began the new friend, with a sympathetic glance.

"I know models are paid for sitting; did you wish to do it with me because I'm poor?" asked Jessie, with an irrepressible frown and a glance at the thrice-cleaned dress and the neatly mended gloves.

Mr. Vane knew what thorn pricked the sensitive little girl, and answered in his friendliest tone:

"I never thought of such a thing. I wanted *you* to help me, because I am poor in what artists so much need — real grace and beauty. I hoped you would allow me to give your sister a copy of the sketch as a token of my gratitude for your great kindness."

The frown vanished and the smile returned as the soft answer turned away Jessie's wrath and made her hasten to say penitently:

"I was very rude; but I haven't learned to be humble yet, and often forget that I am poor. Please come to us any time. Laura will enjoy seeing your work, and be delighted with anything you give her. So shall I, though I don't deserve it."

"I won't punish you by painting the frown that quite frightened me just now, but do my best to keep the happy face, and so heap coals of fire on your head. They won't burn any more than the pretty red leaves that brought me this good fortune," answered the artist, seeing that his peace was made.

"I'm *so* glad I wore them!" and as if trying to make amends for her little flash of temper, Jessie told him about the ivy, and how she loved it — unconsciously betraying more of her pathetic little story than she knew, and increasing her hearer's interest in his new model.

The children came back in riotous spirits, and Jessie was called to lead the revels again. But now her heart was as light as her heels; for she had something pleasant to think of — a hope of help for Laura, and the memory of kind words to make hard duties easier. Mr. Vane soon slipped away, promising to come the next day; and at eight o'clock Jessie ran home to tell her sister the good news, and to press the little wreath which had served her so well.

With the sanguine spirit of girlhood, she felt sure that something delightful would happen, and built fine castles in the air for her sister, with a small corner for herself, where she could watch Laura bloom into a healthy woman and a great artist. The desire of Jessie's heart was to earn enough money to enable them to spend a month or two at the seashore when summer came, as that was the surest cure for Laura's weak nerves and muscles. She had cherished the wild idea of being a ballet-girl, as dancing was her delight; but everyone frowned upon that plan, and her own refined nature told her that it was not the life for a young girl. Mr. Vane's request for her head suggested a splendid hope; and after getting angry with him for hinting at her being a model, she suddenly decided to try it — with the charming inconsistency of her sex. The more she thought of it, the better she liked the idea, and resolved to ask her new friend all about it, fondly hoping that much money could be made in this way.

She said nothing to her sister, but while she sat patiently to Mr. Vane when he came next day she asked many questions; and though somewhat discouraged by his replies, confided to him her hopes and begged his advice. Being a wise man as well as a good and kindly one, he saw at once that his life would not be safe for the pretty, impulsive, and tenderly reared girl, left so unprotected in a world full of trials and temptations. So he told her it would not do, except so far as she would allow him to make several studies of her head in various characters and pay for them.

She consented, and though much disappointed found some consolation in hoarding a part of the handsome sum so earned for the desire of her heart.

The artist seemed in no haste to finish his work, and for some weeks came often to the sittings in that quiet room; for it grew more and more attractive to him, and while he painted the younger sister's changeful face he studied the beautiful nature of the elder and learned to love it. But no one guessed that secret for a long time; and Jessie was so busy racking her brain for a way to earn more money that she was as blind and deaf to much that went on before her as if she had been a wooden dummy.

Suddenly, when she least expected it, help came, and in such a delightful way that she long remembered the little episode with girlish satisfaction. One day as she sat wearily waiting till the dressing-room was cleared of maids and children after the dancing class was over, a former friend came sauntering up to her, saying in the tone which always nettled Jessie:

"You poor thing! Aren't you tired to death trying to teach these stupid babies?"

"No; I love to dance, and we had new figures today. See! Isn't this pretty?" and Jessie, who knew her own skill and loved to display it, twirled away as lightly as if her feet were not aching with two hours of hard work.

"Lovely! I do wish I ever could learn to keep time and not jerk and bounce. Being plump is a dreadful trial," sighed Fanny Fletcher, as Jessie came back beaming and breathless.

"Perhaps I can teach you. I think of making this my profession since I must do something. Mademoiselle earns heaps of money by it," she said, sitting down to rest, resolved not to be ashamed of her work or to let Fanny pity her.

"I wish you *could* teach me, for I know I shall disgrace myself at the Kirmess. You've heard about it, of course? So sorry you can't take a part, for it's going to be great fun and very splendid. I am in the Hungarian dance, and it's one of the hardest; but the dress is lovely, and I would be in it. Mamma is the matron of it; so I had my way, though I know the girls don't want me, and the boys make fun of me. Just see if this isn't the queerest step you ever beheld!"

Fanny started bravely across the wide smooth floor, with a stamp, a slide, and a twirl which was certainly odd, but might have been lively and graceful if she had not unfortunately been a very plump, awkward girl, with no more elasticity than a feather bed. Jessie found it impossible not to laugh when Fanny ended her display with a sprawl upon the floor, and sat rubbing her elbows in an attitude of despair.

"I know that dance! It is the tzardas, and I can show you how it should be done. Jump up and try it with me!" she said good-naturedly, running to help her friend up, glad to have a partner of her own size for once.

Away they went, but soon stopped; for Fanny could not keep step, and Jessie pulled and stamped and hummed in vain.

"Do it alone; then I can see how it goes, and manage better next time," panted the poor girl, dropping down upon the velvet seat which ran round the hall.

Mademoiselle had come in and watched them for a moment. She saw at once what was needed, and as Mrs. Fletcher was one of her best patrons, she was glad to oblige the oldest daughter; so she went to the piano and struck up the proper air just as Jessie, with one arm on her hip, the other on the shoulder of an invisible part-ner, went down the hall with a martial stamp, a quick slide, and a graceful turn, in perfect time to the stirring music that made her nerves tingle and her feet fly. To and fro, round and round, with all manner of graceful gestures, intricate steps, and active bounds went the happy girl, quite carried away by the music and motion of the pastime she loved so much.

Fanny clapped her hands with admiration, and Mademoiselle cried, "Bien, très bien, charmante, ma chérie!" as she paused at last, rosy and smiling, with one hand on her heart and the other at her temple with the salute that closed the dance.

"I *must* learn it! Do come and give me lessons at our house. I called for Maud and must go now. Will you come, Jessie? I'll be glad to pay you if you don't mind. I hate to be laughed at; and I know if someone would just help me alone I should do as well as the rest, for Professor Ludwig raves at us all."

Fanny seemed in such a sad strait, and Jessie sympathized so heartily with her, that she could not refuse a request which flattered her vanity and tempted her with a prospect of some addition to the "Sister-fund," as she called her little savings. So she graciously consented, and after a few laborious lessons prospered so well that her grateful pupil proposed to several other unsuccessful dancers in the set to invite Jessie to the private rehearsals held in various parlors as the festival drew near.

Some of these young people knew Jessie Delano, had missed the bright girl, and gladly welcomed her back when, after much persuasion, she agreed to go and help them with the difficult figures of the tzardas. Once among them she felt in her element, and trained the awkward squad so well that Professor Ludwig complimented them on their improvement at the public rehearsals, and raved no more, to the great delight of the timid damsels, who lost their wits when the fiery little man shouted and wrung his hands over their mistakes.

The young gentlemen needed help also, as several of them looked very much like galvanized grasshoppers in their efforts to manage long legs or awkward elbows. Jessie willingly danced with them, and showed them how to move with grace and spirit, and handle their partners less like dolls and more like peasant maidens with whom the martial Hungarians were supposed to be disporting themselves at the fair. Merry meetings were these; and all enjoyed them, as young people do whatever is lively, dramatic, and social. Everyone was full of the brilliant Kirmess, which was the talk of the city, and to which everyone intended to go as actor or spectator. Jessie was sadly tempted to spend three of her cherished dollars for a ticket, and perhaps would have done so if there had been anyone to take care of her. Laura could not go, and Mr. Vane was away; no other friend appeared, and no one remembered to invite her, so she bravely hid her girlish longing, and got all the pleasure out of the rehearsals that she could.

At the last of these, which was a full-dress affair at Fanny's house, something happened which not only tried Jessie's temper sorely, but brought her a reward for many small sacrifices. So much dancing was very hard upon her slippers, the new pair were worn out long ago, and a second pair were in a dangerous condition; but Jessie hoped that they would last that evening, and then she would indulge in better ones with what Fanny would pay her. She hated to take it, but her salary at Mademoiselle's was needed at home; all she could spare from other sources was sacredly kept for Laura's jaunt, and only now and then did the good little girl buy some very necessary article for herself. She was learning to be humble, to love work, and be grateful for her small wages for her sister's sake; and while she hid her trials, withstood her temptations, and bravely tugged away at her hard tasks, the kind Providence, who teaches us the sweetness of adversity, was preparing a more beautiful and helpful surprise than any she could plan or execute.

That night all were much excited, and great was the energy displayed as the scarlet, blue, and silver couples went through the rapid figures with unusual spirit and success. The brass-heeled boots stamped in perfect time, the furred caps waved, and the braided jackets glittered as the gay troop swung to and fro or marched to the barbaric music of an impromptu band. Jessie looked on with such longing in her eyes that Fanny, who was ill with a bad cold, kindly begged her to take her place, as motion made her cough, and putting on the red and silver cap sent her joyfully away to lead them all.

The fun grew rather fast and furious toward the end, and when the dance broke up there lay in the middle of the floor a shabby little slipper, burst at the side, trodden down at the heel, and utterly demoralized as to the bow with a broken buckle in it. Such a disreputable little shoe was it that no one claimed it when one of the young men held it up on the point of his sword, exclaiming gaily:

"Where is Cinderella? Here's her shoe, and it's quite time she had a new pair. Glass evidently doesn't wear well nowadays."

They all laughed and looked about to find the shoeless foot. The girls with small feet displayed them readily; those less blessed hid them at once, and no Cinderella appeared to claim the old slipper. Jessie turned as red as her cap, and glanced imploringly at Fanny as she slipped through a convenient door and flew upstairs, knowing that in a moment all would see that it must be hers, since the other girls wore red boots as a part of their costume.

Fanny understood; and though awkward and slow with her feet, she was kind-hearted and quick to spare her friend the mortification which a poor and proud girl could not help feeling at such a moment. The unfortunate slipper was flying from hand to hand as the youths indulged in a boyish game of ball to tease the laughing girls, who hastened to disclaim all knowledge of "the horrid thing."

"Please give it to me!" cried Fanny, trying to catch it, and glad Jessie was safe.

"No; Cinderella must come and put it on. Here's the Prince all ready to help her," said the finder of the shoe, holding it up.

"And here are lots of proud sisters to cut off their toes and heels if they could only get on such a small slipper," added another young Magyar, enjoying the fun immensely.

"Listen, and let me tell you something. It's Jessie Delano's, and she has run away because she lost it. Don't laugh and make fun of it, because it was worn out in helping us. You all know what a hard time she has had, but you don't know how good and brave and patient she is, trying to help poor Laura and to earn her living. I asked her to teach me, and I shall pay her well for it, because

I couldn't have gone on if she hadn't. If any of you feel as grateful as I do, and as sorry for her, you can show it in any kind way you please, for it must be dreadful to be so poor."

Fanny had spoken quickly, and at the last words hid the tremble in her voice with a cough, being rather scared at what she had done on the impulse of the moment. But it was a true impulse, and the generous young hearts were quick to answer it. The old slipper was respectfully handed to her with many apologies and various penitent suggestions. None were adopted just then, however, for Fanny ran off to find Jessie with her things on waiting for a chance to slip away unseen. No persuasions would keep her to supper; and at last, with many thanks, she was allowed to go, while Fanny returned to lay plans with her guests as they disturbed their digestions with lobster salad, ice cream, and strong coffee.

Feeling more than ever like Cinderella as she hurried out into the winter night, leaving all the good times behind her, Jessie stood waiting for a car on the windy street corner, with the ragged slippers under her arm, tears of weariness and vexation in her eyes, and a resentful feeling against an unjust fate lying heavy at her heart. The glimpses of her old gay, easy life, which these rehearsals had given her, made the real hardship and loneliness of her present life all the more irksome, and that night she felt as if she could not bear it much longer. She longed with all a girl's love of gaiety to go to the Kirmess, and no one thought to invite her. She could not go alone even if she yielded to temptation and spent her own money. Laura would have to hire a carriage if she ventured to try it; so it was impossible, for six or seven dollars was a fortune to the poor girls now. To have been one of the happy creatures who were to take part in it, to dance on the green in a dainty costume to the music of a full band — to see and do and enjoy all the delights of those two enchanting evenings, would have filled Jessie's cup to overflowing. But since she might as well cry for the moon she tried to get some comfort out of imagining it all as she rumbled home in a snowstorm, and cried herself to sleep after giving Laura a cheerful account of the rehearsal, omitting the catastrophe.

The sun shone next morning, hope woke again, and as she dressed Jessie sang to keep her heart up, still trusting that someone would remember her before the day was over. As she opened her windows the sparrows welcomed her with shrill chirpings, and the sun turned the snow-covered vine to a glittering network very beautiful to see as it hung like a veil of lace over the dingy wall. Jessie smiled as she saw it, while taking a long breath of the keen air, feeling cheered and refreshed by these familiar comforters; then with a brave, bright glance up at the clear blue sky she went away to the day's duties, little guessing what pleasant surprises were on their way to reward her for the little sacrifices which were teaching her strength, patience, and courage for greater ones by and by.

All the morning she listened eagerly for the bell, but nothing came; and at two o'clock she went away to the dancing class, saying to herself with a sigh:

"Everyone is so busy, it is no wonder I'm forgotten. I shall hear about the fun in the papers, and try to be contented with that."

Though she never felt less like dancing, she was very patient with her little pupils, and when the lesson was over sat resting a moment, with her head still full of the glories of the Kirmess.

Suddenly Mademoiselle came to her, and in a few kind words gave her the first of the pleasant surprises by offering her a larger salary, an older class, and many commendations for her skill and faithfulness. Of course she gratefully accepted the welcome offer, and hurried home to tell Laura, forgetting her heavy heart, tired feet, and disappointed hopes.

At her own door the second surprise stood waiting for her, in the person of Mrs. Fletcher's servant with a large box and a note from Miss Fanny. How she ever got herself and her parcel up the long stairs Jessie never knew, she was in such a frantic hurry to see what that vast box could contain. She startled her sister by bursting into the room breathless, flushed, and beaming, with the mysterious cry of:

"Scissors! Quick, the scissors!"

Off went cords and papers, up flew the cover, and with a shriek of rapture Jessie saw the well-known Hungarian costume lying there before her. What it all meant she could not guess, till she tore open the note and read these delightful words:

DEAR JESS,

My cold is worse, and the doctor won't let me go tonight. Isn't it dreadful? Our dance will be ruined unless you will take my place. I know you will to oblige us, and have a lovely time. Everyone will be glad, you do it so much better than I can. My dress will fit you, with tucks and reefs here and there; and the boots won't be much too large, for though I'm fat I have small feet, thank goodness! Mamma will call for you at seven, and bring you safely home; and you must come early tomorrow and tell me all about it.

In the small box you will find a little token of our gratitude to you for your kindness in helping us all so much.

Yours ever,

FAN

As soon as Jessie could get her breath and recover from this first delightful shock, she opened the dainty parcel carefully tied up with pink ribbons. It proved to be a crystal slipper, apparently full of rosebuds; but under the flowers lay five-and-twenty shining gold dollars. A little card with these words was tucked in one corner, as if, with all their devices to make the offering as delicate and pretty as possible, the givers feared to offend:

We return to our dear Princess the glass slipper which she lost at the ball, full of thanks and good wishes.

If the kind young persons who sent the fanciful gift could have seen how it was received, their doubts would soon have been set at rest; for Jessie laughed and cried as she told the story, counted the precious coins, and filled the pretty shoe with water that the buds might keep fresh for Laura. Then, while the needles flew and the gay garments were fitted, the happy voices talked and the sisters rejoiced together over this unexpected pleasure as only loving girls could do.

"The sweetest part of all the splendid surprise is that they remembered me just at the busiest time, and thanked me in such a lovely way. I shall keep that glass slipper all my life, if I can, to remind me not to despair; for just when everything seemed darkest, all this good luck came," said Jessie, with ecstatic skips as she clanked the brass heels of her boots and thought of the proud moment when she would join in the tzardas before all Boston.

Gentle Laura rejoiced and sympathized heartily, sewed like a busy bee, and sent her happy sister away at seven o'clock with her sweetest smile, never letting her suspect what tender hopes and fears were hidden in her own heart, what longing and disappointment made her days doubly sad and lonely, or how very poor a consolation all the glories of the Kirmess would be for the loss of a friend who had grown very near and dear to her.

No need to tell the raptures of that evening to little Jessie, who enjoyed every moment, played her part well, and was brought home at midnight ready to begin all over again, so inexhaustible is youth's appetite for pleasure.

To her great surprise, Laura was up and waiting to welcome her, with a face so full of a new and lovely happiness that Jessie guessed at once some good fortune had come to her also. Yes, Laura's well-earned reward and beautiful surprise had arrived at last; and she told it all in a few words as she held out her arms exclaiming:

"He has come back! He loves me, and I am so happy! Dear little sister, all your hard times are over now, and you shall have a home again."

So the dreams came true, as they sometimes do even in this workaday world of ours, when the dreamers strive as well as hope, and earn their rewards.

Laura had a restful summer at the seaside, with a stronger arm than Jessie's to lean upon, and more magical medicine to help her back to health than any mortal doctor could prescribe. Jessie danced again with a light heart — for pleasure, not for pay — and found the new life all the sweeter for the trials of the old one. In the autumn there was a quiet wedding, before three very happy people sailed away to Italy, the artist's heaven on earth.

"No roses for me," said Jessie, smiling at herself in the mirror as she fastened a spray of rosy ivy leaves in the bosom of her fresh white gown that October morning. "I'll be true to my old friend; for it helped me in my dark days, and now it shall rejoice with me in my bright ones, and go on teaching me to climb bravely and patiently toward the light."

MY RED CAP

from *Proverb Stories*, 1868

The soldier who is the central figure in this story is evidently patterned after someone Louisa took care of in the days when she was a nurse in an army hospital in Washington during the Civil War. He must have impressed her especially for he appears in two of her stories, in the following one and in "Mayflowers" in A Garland for Girls. *Wherever she went she was active in the charitable and benevolent organizations of her day. People in Boston, where she spent so much of her time, recognized that following the Civil War, the United States Government was doing far too little in the way of caring for the wounded and crippled soldiers who had lived through their army service but would never be able to work again. Many men had given their lives, but these pitiful survivors had given their futures to the great cause of putting an end to slavery. The Soldiers' Home in Boston was being established out of voluntary subscription, and it was to support and promote this undertaking that Louisa wrote this story in 1880. Under its title she wrote: "He who serves well need not fear to ask his wages."*

MY RED CAP

I

It was under a blue cap that I first saw the honest face of Joe Collins. In the third year of the late war a Maine regiment was passing through Boston, on its way to Washington. The Common was all alive with troops and the spectators who clustered round them to say God-speed, as the brave fellows marched away to meet danger and death for our sakes.

Everyone was eager to do something; and as the men stood at ease the people mingled freely with them, offering gifts, hearty grips of the hand, and hopeful prophecies of victory in the end. Irresistibly attracted, my boy Tom and I drew near, and soon, becoming excited by the scene, ravaged the fruit stands in our neighborhood for tokens of our regard, mingling candy and congratulations, peanuts and prayers, apples and applause in one enthusiastic jumble.

While Tom was off on his third raid, my attention was attracted be a man who stood a little apart, looking as if his thoughts were far away. All the men were fine, stalwart fellows, as Maine men usually are; but this one overtopped his comrades, standing straight and tall as a Norway pine, with a face full of the mingled shrewdness, sobriety, and self-possession of the typical New Englander. I liked the look of him; and seeing that he seemed solitary even in a crowd, I offered him my last apple with a word of interest. The keen blue eyes met mine gratefully, and the apple began to vanish in vigorous bites as we talked; for no one thought of ceremony at such a time.

"Where are you from?"

"Woolwich, ma'am."

"Are you glad to go?"

"Wal, there's two sides to that question. I calk'late to do my duty, and do it hearty; but it *is* rough on a feller leavin' his folks, for good, maybe."

There was a sudden huskiness in the man's voice that was not apple skins, though he tried to make believe that it was. I knew a word about home would comfort him, so I went on with my questions.

"It is very hard. Do you leave a family?"

"My old mother, a sick brother — and Lucindy."

The last word was uttered in a tone of intense regret, and his brown cheek reddened as he added hastily, to hide some embarrassment:

"You see, Jim went last year, and got pretty well used up; so I felt as if I'd ought to take my turn now. Mother was a regular old hero about it, and I dropped everything and come off. Lucindy didn't think it was my duty; and that made it awful hard, I tell you."

"Wives are less patriotic than mothers," I began; but he would not hear Lucindy blamed, and said quickly:

"She ain't my wife yet, but we calk'lated to be married in a month or so; and it was wus for her than for me, women lot so on not being disappointed. I *couldn't* shirk, and here I be. When I git to work, I shall be all right: the first wrench is the tryin' part."

Here he straightened his broad shoulders and turned his face toward the flags fluttering far in front, as if no backward look should betray the longing of his heart for mother, home, and wife. I liked that little glimpse of character; and when Tom returned with empty hands, reporting that every stall was exhausted, I told him to find out what the man would like best, then run across the street and get it.

"I know without asking. Give us your purse, and I'll make him as happy as a king," said the boy, laughing, as he looked up admiringly at our tall friend, who looked down on him with an elder-brotherly air pleasant to see. While Tom was gone, I found out Joe's name and business, promised to write and tell his mother how finely the regiment went off, and was just expressing a hope that we might meet again, for I too was going to the war as nurse, when the order to "Fall in!" came rolling down the ranks, and the talk was over. Fearing Tom would miss our man in the confusion, I kept my eye on him till the boy came rushing up with a packet of tobacco in one hand and a good supply of cigars in the other. Not a romantic offering, certainly, but a very acceptable one, as Joe's face proved, as we scrambled these treasures into his pockets, all laughing at the flurry, while less fortunate comrades helped us, with an eye to a share of these fragrant luxuries by and by. There was just time for this, a hearty shake of the big hand, and a grateful "Good-by, ma'am," — then the word was given, and they were off. Bent on seeing the last of them, Tom and I took a short cut, and came out on the wide street down which so many troops marched that year; and, mounting some high steps, we watched for our man, as we already called him.

As the inspiring music, the grand tramp, drew near, the old thrill went through the crowd, the old cheer broke out. But it was a different scene now than in the first enthusiastic, hopeful days. Young men and ardent boys filled the ranks then, brave by instinct, burning with loyal zeal, and blissfully unconscious of all that lay before them. Now the blue coats were worn by mature men, some gray, all grave and resolute: husbands and fathers, with the memory of wives and children tugging at their heartstrings; homes left desolate behind them, and before them the grim certainty of danger, hardship, and perhaps the lifelong helplessness worse than death. Little of the glamour of romance about the war now: they saw it as it was, a long, hard task; and here were the men to do it well. Even the lookers-on were different now. Once all was wild enthusiasm and glad uproar; now men's lips were set, and women's smileless as they cheered; fewer handkerchiefs whitened the air, for wet eyes needed them; and sudden lulls, almost solemn in their stillness, followed the acclamations of the crowd. All watched with quickened breath and brave souls that living wave, blue below, and bright with a steely glitter above, as it flowed down the street and away to distant battlefields already stained with precious blood.

"There he is! The outside man, and tallest of the lot. Give him a cheer, auntie: he sees us, and remembers!" cried Tom, nearly tumbling off his perch as he waved his hat and pointed out Joe Collins.

Yes, there he was, looking up, with a smile on his brave brown face, my little nosegay in his buttonhole, a suspicious bulge in the pocket close by, and doubtless a comfortable quid in his mouth, to cheer the weary march. How like an old friend he looked, though we had only met fifteen minutes ago; how glad we were to be there to smile back at him, and send him on his way feeling that even in a strange city there was someone to say, "God bless you, Joe!" We watched the tallest blue cap till it vanished, and then went home in a glow of patriotism — Tom to long for his turn to come, I to sew vigorously on the gray gown the new nurse burned to wear as soon as possible, and both of us to think and speak often of poor Joe Collins and his Lucindy. All this happened long ago; but it is well to recall those stirring times — to keep fresh the memory of sacrifices made for us by men like these; to see to it that the debt we owe them is honestly, gladly paid; and, while we decorate the graves of those who died, to remember also those who still live to deserve our grateful care.

II

I never expected to see Joe again; but, six months later, we did meet in a Washington hospital one winter's night. A train of ambulances had left their sad freight at our door, and we were hurrying to get the poor fellows into much needed beds, after a week of hunger, cold, and unavoidable neglect. All forms of pain were in my ward that night, and all borne with the pathetic patience which was a daily marvel to those who saw it.

Trying to bring order out of chaos, I was rushing up and down the narrow aisle between the rows of rapidly filling beds, and, after brushing several times against a pair of the largest and muddiest boots I ever saw, I paused at last to inquire why they were impeding the passageway. I found they belonged to a very tall man who seemed to be already asleep or dead, so white and still and utterly worn-out he looked as he lay there, without a coat, a great patch on his forehead, and the right arm rudely bundled up. Stooping to cover him, I saw that he was unconscious, and, whipping out my brandy bottle and salts, soon brought him round, for it was only exhaustion.

"Can you eat?" I asked, as he said, "Thanky, ma'am," after a long draught of water and a dizzy stare.

"Eat! I'm starvin'!" he answered, with such a ravenous glance at a fat nurse who happened to be passing that I trembled for her, and hastened to take a bowl of soup from her tray.

As I fed him, his gaunt, weather-beaten face had a familiar look; but so many such faces had passed before me that winter, I did not recall this one till the ward-master came to put up the cards with the newcomers' names above their beds. My man seemed absorbed in his food; but I naturally glanced at the card, and there was the name "Joseph Collins" to give me an additional interest in my new patient.

"Why, Joe! Is it really you?" I exclaimed, pouring the last spoonful of soup down his throat so hastily that I choked him.

"All that's left of me. Wal, ain't this luck, now?" gasped Joe, as gratefully as if that hospital cot was a bed of roses.

"What is the matter? A wound in the head and arm?" I asked, feeling sure that no slight affliction had brought Joe there.

"Right arm gone. Shot off as slick as a whistle. I tell you, it's a sing'lar kind of a feelin' to see a piece of your own body go flyin' away, with no prospect of ever coming back again," said Joe, trying to make light of one of the greatest misfortunes a man can suffer.

"That is bad, but it might have been worse. Keep up your spirits, Joe; and we will soon have you fitted out with a new arm almost as good as new."

"I guess it won't do much lumberin', so that trade is done for. I s'pose there's things left-handed fellers can do, and I must learn 'em as soon as possible, since my fightin' days are over," and Joe looked at his one arm with a sigh that was almost a groan, helplessness is such a trial to a manly man — and he was eminently so.

"What can I do to comfort you most, Joe? I'll send my good Ben to help you to bed, and will be here myself when the surgeon goes his rounds. Is there anything else that would make you more easy?"

"If you could just drop a line to mother to let her know I'm alive, it would be a sight of comfort to both of us. I guess I'm in for a long spell of hospital, and I'd lay easier if I knew mother and Lucindy warn't frettin' about me."

He must have been suffering terribly, but he thought of the women who loved him before himself, and busy as I was, I snatched a moment to send a few words of hope to the old mother. Then I left him "layin' easy," though the prospect of some months of wearing pain would have daunted most men. If I had needed anything to increase my regard for Joe, it would have been the courage with which he bore a very bad quarter of an hour with the surgeons; for his arm was in a dangerous state, the wound in the head feverish for want of care; and a heavy cold on the lungs suggested pneumonia as an added trial to his list of ills.

"He will have a hard time of it, but I think he will pull through, as he is a temperate fellow, with a splendid constitution," was the doctor's verdict, as he left us for the next man, who was past help, with a bullet through his lungs.

"I don'no as I hanker to live, and be a burden. If Jim was able to do for mother, I feel as if I wouldn't mind steppin' out, now I'm so fur along. As he ain't, I s'pose I must brace up and do the best I can," said Joe, as I wiped the drops from his forehead, and tried to look as if his prospect was a bright one.

"You will have Lucindy to help you, you know; and that will make things easier for all."

"Think so? 'Pears to me I couldn't ask her to take care of three invalids for my sake. She ain't no folks of her own, nor much means, and ought to marry a man who can make things easy for her. Guess I'll have to wait a spell longer before I say anything to Lucindy about marryin' now," and a look of resolute resignation settled on Joe's haggard face as he gave up his dearest hope.

"I think Lucindy will have something to say, if she is like most women, and you will find the burdens much lighter, for sharing them between you. Don't worry about that, but get well, and go home as soon as you can."

"All right, ma'am," and Joe proved himself a good soldier by obeying orders and falling asleep like a tired child, as the first step toward recovery.

For two months I saw Joe daily, and learned to like him very much, he was so honest, genuine, and kind-hearted. So did his mates, for he made friends with them all by sharing such small luxuries as came to him, for he was a favorite; and, better still, he made sunshine in that sad place by the brave patience with which he bore his own troubles, the cheerful consolation he always gave to others. A droll fellow was Joe at times, for under his sobriety lay much humor; and I soon discovered that a visit from him was more efficacious than other cordials in cases of despondency and discontent. Roars of laughter sometimes greeted me as I went into his ward, and Joe's jokes were passed round as eagerly as the water pitcher.

Yet he had much to try him, not only in the ills that vexed his flesh, but the cares that tried his spirit and the future that lay before him, full of anxieties and responsibilities which seemed so heavy now when the strong right arm, that had cleared all obstacles away before, was gone. The letters I wrote for him, and those he received, told the little story very plainly; for he read them to me, and found much comfort in talking over his affairs, as most men do when illness makes them dependent on a woman. Jim was evidently sick and selfish. Lucindy, to judge from the photograph cherished so tenderly under Joe's pillow, was a pretty, weak sort of a girl, with little character or courage to help poor Joe with his burdens. The old mother was very like her son, and stood by him "like a hero," as he said, but was evidently failing, and begged him to come home as soon as he was able, that she might see him comfortably settled before she must leave him. Her courage sustained his, and the longing to see her hastened his departure as soon as it was safe to let him go; for Lucindy's letters were always of a dismal sort, and made him anxious to put his shoulder to the wheel.

"She always set consid'able by me, mother did, bein' the oldest; and I wouldn't miss makin' her last days happy, not if it cost me all the arms and legs I've got," said Joe, as he awkwardly struggled into the big boots an hour after leave to go home was given him.

It was pleasant to see his comrades gather round him with such hearty adieus that his one hand must have tingled; to hear the good wishes and the thanks called after him by pale creatures in their beds; and to find tears in many eyes besides my own when he was gone, and nothing was left of him but the empty cot, the old gray wrapper, and the name upon the wall.

I kept that card among my other relics, and hoped to meet Joe again somewhere in the world. He sent me one or two letters, then I went home; the war ended soon after, time passed, and the little story of my Maine lumberman was laid away with many other experiences which made that part of my life a very memorable one.

III

Some years later, as I looked out of my window one dull November day, the only cheerful thing I saw was the red cap of a messenger who was examining the slate that hung on a wall opposite my hotel. A tall man with gray hair and beard, one arm, and a blue army coat. I always salute, figuratively at least, when I see that familiar blue, especially if one sleeve of the coat is empty; so I watched the messenger with interest as he trudged away on some new errand, wishing he had a better day and a thicker pair of boots. He was an unusually large, well-made man, and reminded me of a fine building going to ruin before its time; for the broad shoulders were bent, there was a stiffness about the long legs suggestive of wounds or rheumatism, and the curly hair looked as if snow had fallen on it too soon. Sitting at work in my window, I fell into the way of watching my Red Cap, as I called him, with more interest than I did the fat doves on the roof opposite, or the pert sparrows hopping in the mud below. I liked the steady way in which he plodded on through fair weather or foul, as if intent on doing well the one small service he had found to do. I liked his cheerful whistle as he stood waiting for a job under the porch of the public building where his slate hung, watching the luxurious carriages roll by, and the well-to-do gentlemen who daily passed him to their comfortable homes, with a steady, patient sort of face, as if wondering at the inequalities of fortune, yet neither melancholy nor morose over the small share of prosperity which had fallen to his lot.

I often planned to give him a job, that I might see him nearer; but I had few errands, and little Bob, the hall-boy, depended on doing those: so the winter was nearly over before I found out that my Red Cap was an old friend.

A parcel came for me one day, and bidding the man wait for an answer, I sat down to write it, while the messenger stood just inside the door like a sentinel on duty. When I looked up to give my note and directions, I found the man staring at me with a beaming yet bashful face, as he nodded, saying heartily:

"I mistrusted it was you, ma'am, soon's I see the name on the bundle, and I guess I ain't wrong. It's a number of years sense we met, and you don't remember Joe Collins as well as he does you, I reckon?"

"Why, how you have changed! I've been seeing you every day all winter, and never knew you," I said, shaking hands with my old patient, and very glad to see him.

"Nigh on to twenty years makes consid'able of a change in folks, 'specially if they have a pretty hard row to hoe."

"Sit down and warm yourself while you tell me all about it; there is no hurry for this answer, and I'll pay for your time."

Joe laughed as if that was a good joke, and sat down as if the fire was quite as welcome as the friend.

"How are they all at home?" I asked, as he sat turning his cap around, not quite knowing where to begin.

"I haven't got any home nor any folks neither," and the melancholy words banished the brightness from his rough face like a cloud. "Mother died soon after I got back. Suddin, but she was ready, and I was there, so she was happy. Jim lived a number of years, and was a sight of care, poor feller; but we managed to rub along, though we had to sell the farm: for I couldn't do much with one arm, and doctor's bills right along stiddy take a heap of money. He was as comfortable as he could be; and when he was gone it wasn't no great matter, for there was only me, and I don't mind roughin' it."

"But Lucindy, where was she?" I asked very naturally.

"Oh! She married another man long ago. Couldn't expect her to take me and my misfortins. She's doin' well, I hear, and that's a comfort anyway."

There was a look on Joe's face, a tone in Joe's voice as he spoke, that plainly showed how much he had needed comfort when left to bear his misfortunes all alone. But he made no complaint, uttered no reproach, and loyally excused Lucindy's desertion with a simple sort of dignity that made it impossible to express pity or condemnation.

"How came you here, Joe?" I asked, making a sudden leap from past to present.

"I had to scratch for a livin', and can't do much; so, after tryin' a number of things, I found this. My old wounds pester me a good deal, and rheumatism is bad winters; but while my legs hold out, I can git on. A man can't set down and starve; so I keep waggin' as long as I can. When I can't do no more, I s'pose there's almshouse and hospital ready for me."

"That is a dismal prospect, Joe. There ought to be a comfortable place for such as you to spend your last days in. I am sure you have earned it."

"Wal, it does seem ruther hard on us when we've give all we had, and give it free and hearty, to be left to knock about in our old age. But there's so many poor folks to be took care of, we don't get much of a chance, for *we* ain't the beggin' sort," said Joe, with a wistful look at the wintry world outside, as if it would be better to lie quiet under the snow than to drag out his last painful years, friendless and forgotten, in some refuge of the poor.

"Some kind people have been talking of a home for soldiers, and I hope the plan will be carried out. It will take time; but if it comes to pass, you shall be one of the first men to enter that home, Joe, if I can get you there."

"That sounds mighty cheerin' and comfortable, thanky, ma'am. Idleness is dreadful tryin' to me, and I'd ruther wear out than rust out; so I guess I can weather it a spell longer. But it will be pleasant to look forrard to a snug harbor bymeby. I feel a sight better just hearin' tell about it." He certainly looked so, faint as the hope was; for the melancholy eyes brightened as if they already saw a happier refuge in the future than almshouse, hospital, or grave, and when he trudged away upon my errand he went as briskly as if every step took him nearer to the promised home.

After that day it was all up with Bob, for I told my neighbors Joe's story, and we kept him trotting busily, adding little gifts, and taking the sort of interest in him that comforted the lonely fellow, and made him feel that he had not outlived his usefulness. I never looked out when he was at his post that he did not smile back at me; I never passed him in the street that the red cap was not touched with a military flourish; and when any of us beckoned to him, no twinge of rheumatism was too sharp to keep him from hurrying to do our errands, as if he had Mercury's winged feet.

Now and then he came in for a chat, and always asked how the Soldiers' Home was prospering; expressing his opinion that "Boston was the charitablest city under the sun, and he was sure he and his mates would be took care of somehow."

When we parted in the spring, I told him things looked hopeful, bade him be ready for a good long rest as soon as the hospitable doors were open, and left him nodding cheerfully.

IV

But in the autumn I looked in vain for Joe. The slate was in its old place, and a messenger came and went on his beat; but a strange face was under the red cap, and this man had two arms and one eye. I asked for Collins, but the newcomer had only a vague idea that he was dead; and the same answer was given me at headquarters, though none of the busy people seemed to know when or where he died. So I mourned for Joe, and felt that it was very hard he could not have lived to enjoy the promised refuge;

for, relying upon the charity that never fails, the Home was an actual fact now, just beginning its beneficent career. People were waking up to this duty, money was coming in, meetings were being held, and already a few poor fellows were in the refuge, feeling themselves no longer paupers, but invalid soldiers honorably supported by the State they had served. Talking it over one day with a friend, who spent her life working for the Associated Charities, she said:

"By the way, there is a man boarding with one of my poor women, who ought to be got into the Home, if he will go. I don't know much about him, except that he was in the army, has been very ill with rheumatic fever, and is friendless. I asked Mrs. Flanagin how she managed to keep him, and she said she had help while he was sick, and now he is able to hobble about, he takes care of the children, so she is able to go out to work. He won't go to his own town, because there is nothing for him there but the almshouse, and he dreads a hospital; so struggles along, trying to earn his bread tending babies with his one arm. A sad case, and in your line; I wish you'd look into it."

"That sounds like my Joe, one arm and all. I'll go and see him; I've a weakness for soldiers, sick or well."

I went, and never shall forget the pathetic little tableau I saw as I opened Mrs. Flanagin's dingy door; for she was out, and no one heard my tap. The room was redolent of suds, and in a grove of damp clothes hung on lines sat a man with a crying baby laid across his lap, while he fed three small children standing at his knee with bread and molasses. How he managed with one arm to keep the baby from squirming on to the floor, the plate from upsetting, and to feed the hungry urchins who stood in a row with open mouths, like young birds, was past my comprehension. But he did, trotting baby gently, dealing out sweet morsels patiently, and whistling to himself, as if to beguile his labors cheerfully.

The broad back, the long legs, the faded coat, the low whistle were all familiar; and, dodging a wet sheet, I faced the man to find

it was indeed my Joe! A mere shadow of his former self, after
months of suffering that had crippled him for life, but brave and
patient still; trying to help himself, and not ask aid though
brought so low.

For an instant I could not speak to him, and, encumbered with
baby, dish, spoon, and children, he could only stare at me with a
sudden brightening of the altered face that made it full of welcome
before a word was uttered.

"They told me you were dead, and I only heard of you by acci-
dent, not knowing I should find my old friend alive, but not well,
I'm afraid?"

"There ain't much left of me but bones and pain, ma'am. I'm
powerful glad to see you all the same. Dust off a chair, Patsey, and
let the lady set down. You go in the corner, and take turns lickin'
the dish, while I see company," said Joe, disbanding his small
troop, and shouldering the baby as if presenting arms in honor of
his guest.

"Why didn't you let me know how sick you were? And how
came they to think you dead?" I asked, as he festooned the wet
linen out of the way, and prepared to enjoy himself as best he
could.

"I did send once, when things was at the wust; but you hadn't
got back, and then somehow I thought I was goin' to be mustered
out for good, and so wouldn't trouble nobody. But my orders ain't
come yet, and I am doing the fust thing that come along. It ain't
much, but the good soul stood by me, and I ain't ashamed to pay
my debts this way, sence I can't do it in no other," and Joe cradled
the chubby baby in his one arm as tenderly as if it had been his
own, though little Biddy was not an inviting infant.

"That is very beautiful and right, Joe, and I honor you for it;
but you were not meant to tend babies, so sing your last lullabies,
and be ready to go to the Home as soon as I can get you there."

"Really, ma'am? I used to lay and kind of dream about it when
I couldn't stir without yellin' out; but I never thought it would

ever come to happen. I see a piece in the paper describing it, and it sounded dreadful nice. Shouldn't wonder if I found some of my mates there. They were a good lot, and deservin' of all that could be done for 'em," said Joe, trotting the baby briskly, as if the prospect excited him, as well it might, for the change from that damp nursery to the comfortable quarters prepared for him would be like going from Purgatory to Paradise.

"I don't wonder you don't get well living in such a place, Joe. You should have gone home to Woolwich, and let your friends help you," I said, feeling provoked with him for hiding himself.

"No, ma'am!" he answered, with a look I never shall forget, it was so full of mingled patience, pride, and pain. "I haven't a relation in the world but a couple of poor old aunts, and they couldn't do anything for me. As for asking help of folks I used to know, I couldn't do it; and if you think I'd go to Lucindy, though she is wal off, you don't know Joe Collins. I'd die fust! If she was poor and I rich, I'd do for her like a brother; but I couldn't ask no favors of her, not if I begged my vittles in the street, or starved. I forgive, but I don't forgit in a hurry; and the woman that stood by me when I was down is the woman I believe in, and can take my bread from without shame. Hooray for Biddy Flanagin! God bless her!" and, as if to find a vent for the emotion that filled his eyes with grateful tears, Joe led off the cheer, which the children shrilly echoed, and I joined heartily.

"I shall come for you in a few days; so cuddle the baby and make much of the children before you part. It won't take you long to pack up, will it?" I asked, as we subsided with a general laugh.

"I reckon not, as I don't own any clothes but what I set in, except a couple of old shirts and them socks. My hat's stoppin' up the winder, and my old coat is my bed-cover. I'm awful shabby, ma'am, and that's one reason I don't go out more. I can hobble some, but I ain't got used to bein' a scarecrow yet," and Joe glanced from the hose without heels that hung on the line to the ragged suit he wore, with a resigned expression that made me long to rush out and buy up half the contents of Oak Hall on the spot.

Curbing this wild impulse, I presently departed with promises of speedy transportation for Joe, and unlimited oranges to assuage the pangs of parting for the young Flanagins, who escorted me to the door, while Joe waved the baby like a triumphal banner till I got round the corner.

There was such a beautiful absence of red tape about the new institution that it only needed a word in the right ear to set things going; and then, with a long pull, a strong pull, and a pull all together, Joe Collins was taken up and safely landed in the Home he so much needed and so well deserved.

A happier man or a more grateful one it would be hard to find, and if a visitor wants an enthusiastic guide about the place, Joe is the one to take, for all is comfort, sunshine, and goodwill to him; and he unconsciously shows how great the need of this refuge is, as he hobbles about on his lame feet, pointing out its beauties, conveniences, and delights with his one arm, while his face shines, and his voice quavers a little as he says gratefully:

"The State don't forget us, you see, and this is a Home wuth havin'. Long life to it!"

POPPIES AND WHEAT

from *A Garland for Girls*, 1886

In 1865, when she was over thirty years old, there came to Louisa the opportunity which she had longed for since she was a child, the chance for a journey to Europe. Although the conditions were not ideal, for she was to be companion to an invalid, the experience brought her stimulation and an awakening of the imagination such as she had never had before. In the later months of her stay she was able, finally, to travel by herself, and her sheer delight in seeing all kinds of people and beautiful places and things of which she had so often dreamed made an extraordinary difference to her later writing. Some years after, she went again, this time for a year, with her sister May and a congenial friend. What she got from this happy foreign travel lives again in the background of such stories as this one, where two young girls are taken to Europe to see her favorite places.

POPPIES AND WHEAT

As the great steamer swung round into the stream the cloud of white handkerchiefs waving on the wharf melted away, the last good-byes grew fainter, and those who went and those who stayed felt that the parting was over — "It may be for years, and it may be forever," as the song says.

With only one of the many groups on the deck need we concern ourselves, and a few words will introduce our fellow-travelers. A brisk middle-aged lady leaned on the arm of a middle-aged gentleman in spectacles, both wearing the calmly cheerful air of people used to such scenes, and conscious only of the relief change of place brings to active minds and busy lives.

Before them stood two girls, evidently their charges, and as evidently not sisters, for in all respects they were a great contrast. The younger was a gay creature of seventeen, in an effective costume of navy-blue and white, with bright hair blowing in the wind, sparkling eyes roving everywhere, lively tongue going, and an air of girlish excitement pleasant to see. Both hands were full of farewell bouquets, which she surveyed with more pride than tenderness as she glanced at another group of girls less blessed with floral offerings.

Her companion was a small, quiet person, some years older than herself, very simply dressed, laden with wraps, and apparently conscious just then of nothing but three dark specks on the wharf, as she still waved her little white flag, and looked shoreward with eyes too dim for seeing. A sweet, modest face it was, with intelligent eyes, a firm mouth, and the look of one who had early learned self-reliance and self-control.

The lady and gentleman watched the pair with interest and amusement; for both liked young people, and were anxious to know these two better, since they were to be their guides and guardians for six months. Professor Homer was going abroad to look up certain important facts for his great historical work, and as usual took his wife with him; for they had no family, and the good lady was ready to march to any quarter of the globe at short notice. Fearing to be lonely while her husband pored over old papers in foreign libraries, Mrs. Homer had invited Ethel Amory, a friend's daughter, to accompany her. Of course the invitation was gladly accepted, for it was a rare opportunity to travel in such company, and Ethel was wild with delight at the idea. One thorn, however, vexed her, among the roses with which her way seemed strewn. Mamma would not let her take a French maid, but preferred a young lady as companion; for, three being an awkward number, a fourth party would be not only convenient, but necessary on the girl's account, since she was not used to take care of herself and Mrs. Homer could only be expected to act as chaperone.

"Jane Bassett is just the person I want, and Jane shall go. She needs a change after teaching all these years; it will do her a world of good, for she will improve and enjoy every moment, and the salary I shall offer her will make it worth her while," said Mrs. Amory, as she discussed the plan with her daughter.

"She is only three years older than I am, and I hate to be taken care of, and watched, and fussed over. I can order a maid around, but a companion is worse than a governess; such people are always sensitive and proud, and hard to get on with. Everyone takes a maid, and I'd set my heart on that nice Marie who wants to go home, and talks such lovely French. Do let me have her, Mamma!" begged Ethel, who was a spoiled child and usually got her own way.

But for once Mamma stood firm, having a strong desire to benefit her daughter by the society of better companions than the gay
girls of her own set, also to give a great pleasure to good little Jane
Bassett, who had been governessing ever since she was sixteen,
with very few vacations in her hard, dutiful life.

"No, darling, I have asked Jane, and if her mother can spare
her, Jane it shall be. She is just what you need — sensible and
kind, intelligent and capable; not ashamed to do anything for you,
and able to teach you a great deal in a pleasant way. Mrs. Homer
approves of her, and I am sure you will be glad by and by; for
traveling is not all 'fun,' as you expect, and I don't want you to be a
burden on our friends. You two young things can take care of each
other while the Professor and his wife are busy with their own
affairs; and Jane is a far better companion for you than that co-
quettish French woman, who will probably leave you in the lurch
as soon as you reach Paris. I shouldn't have a moment's peace if
you were left with her, but I have entire confidence in Jane Bassett
because she is faithful, discreet, and a true lady in all things."

There was no more to be said, and Ethel pouted in vain. Jane
accepted the place with joy; and after a month of delightful hurry
they were off, one all eagerness for the new world, the other full of
tender regret for the dear souls left behind. How they got on, and
what they learned, remains to be told.

"Come, Miss Bassett, we can't see them any longer, so we may
as well begin to enjoy ourselves. You might take those things
down below, and settle the stateroom a bit; I'm going to walk
about and get my bearings before lunch. You will find me somewhere around."

Ethel spoke with a little tone of command, having made up her
mind to be mistress and keep Jane Bassett in her place, though she
did know three languages and sketched much better than Miss
Amory.

Jenny, as we who are going to be her bosom friends will call
her, nodded cheerfully, and looked about for the stairway; for,

never having been on a steamer before, she was rather bewildered.

"I'll show you the way, my dear. I always get my things settled at once, as one never knows when one may have to turn in. The Professor will go with you, Ethel; it is not proper for you to roam about alone." And with that hint Mrs. Homer led the way below, privately wondering how these young persons were going to get on together.

Jane swallowed her *heimweh* in silence, and bestirred herself so well that soon the stateroom looked very cozy with the wrappers laid ready, the hanging bags tacked up, and all made shipshape for the ten days' trip.

"But where are *your* comforts? You have given Ethel all the room, the lower berth, and the best of everything," said Mrs. Homer, popping in her head to see how her quiet neighbor got on.

"Oh, I live in my trunk; I didn't bring half as many little luxuries as Ethel did, so I don't need as much room. I'm used to living in corners like a mouse, and I get on very well," answered Jane, looking very like a mouse just then, as she peeped out of the upper berth, with her gray gown, bright eyes, and quick nod of contentment.

"Well, my dear, I've just one word of advice to give you. Don't let that child tyrannize over you. She means well, but is willful and thoughtless, and it is *not* your duty to be made a slave of. Assert yourself and she will obey and respect you, and you will help her a great deal. I know all about it; I was a companion in my youth, and had a hard time of it till I revolted and took my proper place. Now let us go up and enjoy the fine air while we can."

"Thank you, I will remember," and Jane offered the good lady her arm, with a feeling of gratitude for such friendliness, all being new and strange to her, and many doubts of her own fitness for the position lying heavy at her heart.

But soon all was forgotten as she sat on deck watching the islands, lighthouses, ships, and shores glide by as she went swiftly

out to sea that bright June day. Here was the long-cherished desire of her life come to pass at last, and now the parting with
mother and sisters was over, nothing but pleasure remained, and a
very earnest purpose to improve this unexpected opportunity to the
uttermost. The cares of life had begun early for little Jane, she
being the eldest of the three girls, and her mother a widow. First
came hard study, then a timid beginning as nursery governess;
and as year by year the teaching of others taught her, she ventured
on till here she was companion to a fine young lady "going
abroad," where every facility for acquiring languages, studying
history, seeing the best pictures, and enjoying good society would
all be hers. No wonder the quiet face under the modest gray hat
beamed, as it turned wistfully toward the unknown world before
her, and that her thoughts were so far away, she was quite unconscious of the kind eyes watching her, as Mrs. Homer sat placidly
knitting beside her.

"I shall like the Mouse, I'm quite sure. Hope Lemuel will be as
well satisfied. Ethel is charming when she chooses, but will need
looking after, that's plain," thought the lady as she glanced down
the deck to where her husband stood talking with several gentlemen, while his charge was already making friends with the gay
girls who were to be her fellow-passengers.

"Daisy Millers, I fear," went on Mrs. Homer, who had a keen
eye for character, and was as fond of studying the people about
her as the Professor was of looking up dead statesmen, kings, and
warriors. The young ladies certainly bore some resemblance to the
type of American girl which one never fails to meet in traveling.
They were dressed in the height of the fashion, pretty with the
delicate evanescent beauty of too many of our girls, and all gifted
with the loud voices, shrill laughter, and free-and-easy manners
which so astonish decorous English matrons and maids. Ethel
was evidently impressed with their style, as they had a man and
maid at their beck and call, and every sign of ostentatious wealth
about them. A stout papa, a thin mamma, evidently worn out with

the cares of the past winter, three half-grown girls, and a lad of sixteen made up the party; and a very lively one it was, as the Professor soon found, for he presently bowed himself away, and left Ethel to her new friends, since she smilingly refused to leave them.

"Ought I to go to her?" asked Jenny, waking from her happy reverie to a sudden sense of duty as the gentleman sat down beside her.

"Oh dear, no, she is all right. Those are the Sibleys of New York. Her father knows them, and she will find them a congenial refuge when she tires of us quiet folk; and you too, perhaps?" added the Professor as he glanced at the girl.

"I think not. I should not be welcome to them, nor are they the sort of people I like. I shall be very happy with the 'quiet folk,' if they won't let me be in the way," answered Jenny, in the cheerful voice that reminded one of the chirp of a robin.

"We won't; we'll toss you overboard as soon as you begin to scream and bounce in that style," he answered, laughing at the idea of this demure young person's ever dreaming of such a thing. Jenny laughed also, and ran to pick up Mrs. Homer's ball, as it set out for a roll into the lee scuppers. As she brought it back she found the Professor examining the book she left behind her.

"Like all young travelers you cling to your Baedeker, I see, even in the first excitement of the start. He is a useful fellow, but I know my Europe so well now, I don't need him."

"I thought it would be wise to read up our route a little, then I needn't ask questions. They must be very tiresome to people who know all about it," said Jenny, regarding him with an expression of deep respect, for she considered him a sort of walking encyclopedia of universal knowledge.

It pleased the learned man, who was kindly as well as wise, and loved to let his knowledge overflow into any thirsty mind, however small the cup might be. He liked the intelligent face before him, and a timid question or two set him off on his favorite hobby at a pleasant amble, with Jenny on the pillion behind, as it were. She enjoyed it immensely, and was deep in French history when the lunch gong recalled her from Francis I and his sister Margaret to chops and English ale.

Ethel came prancing back to her own party, full of praises of the Sibleys, and the fun they meant to have together.

"They are going to the Langham; so we shall be able to go about with them, and they know all the best shops, and some lords and ladies, and expect to be in Paris when we are, and that will be a great help with our dresses and things."

"But we are not going to shop and have new dresses till we are on our way home, you know. Now we haven't time for such things, and can't trouble the Homers with more trunks," answered Jenny, as they followed their elders to the table.

"I shall buy what I like, and have ten trunks if it suits me. I'm not going to poke round over old books and ruins, and live in a traveling-dress all the time. You can do as you like; it's different with me, and *I* know what is proper."

With which naughty speech Ethel took her seat first at the table, and began to nod and smile at the Sibleys opposite. Jenny set her lips and made no answer, but ate her lunch with what appetite she could, trying to forget her troubles in listening to the chat going on around her.

All that afternoon Ethel left her to herself, and enjoyed the more congenial society of the new acquaintances. Jenny was tired, and glad to read and dream in the comfortable seat Mrs. Homer left her when she went for her nap.

By sunset the sea grew rough and people began to vanish below. There were many empty places at dinnertime, and those who appeared seemed to have lost their appetites suddenly. The Homers were good sailors, but Jenny looked pale, and Ethel said her head ached, though both kept up bravely till nine o'clock, when the Sibleys precipitately retired after supper, and Ethel thought she might as well go to bed early to be ready for another pleasant day tomorrow.

Jenny had a bad night, but disturbed no one. Ethel slept soundly, and sprang up in the morning, eager to be the first on deck. But a sudden lurch sent her and her hairbrush into a corner; and when she rose, everything in the stateroom seemed to be turning somersaults, while a deathly faintness crept over her.

"Oh, wake up, Jane! We are sinking! What is it? Help me, help me!" and with a dismal wail Ethel tumbled into her berth in the first anguish of seasickness.

We will draw the curtain for three days, during which rough weather and general despair reigned. Mrs. Homer took care of the girls till Jenny was able to sit up and amuse Ethel; but the latter had a hard time of it, for a series of farewell lunches had left her in a bad state for a sea-voyage, and the poor girl could not lift her head for days. The new-made friends did not trouble themselves about her after a call of condolence, but faithful Jenny sat by her hour after hour, reading and talking by day, singing her to sleep at night, and often creeping from her bed on the sofa to light her little candle and see that her charge was warmly covered and quite comfortable. Ethel was used to being petted, so she was not very grateful; but she felt the watchful care about her, and thought Jane almost as handy a person as a maid, and told her so.

Jenny thanked her and said nothing of her own discomforts; but Mrs. Homer saw them, and wrote to Mrs. Amory that so far the companion was doing admirably and all that could be desired. A few days later she added more commendations to the journal-letters she kept for the anxious mothers at home, and this serio-comical event was the cause of her fresh praises.

The occupants of the deck staterooms were wakened in the middle of the night by a crash and a cry, and starting up found that the engines were still, and something was evidently the matter somewhere. A momentary panic took place; ladies screamed, children cried, and gentlemen in queer costumes burst out of their rooms, excitedly demanding, "What is the matter?"

As no lamps are allowed in the rooms at night, darkness added to the alarm, and it was some time before the real state of the case was known. Mrs. Homer went at once to the frightened girls, and found Ethel clinging to Jenny, who was trying to find the life preservers lashed to the wall.

"We've struck! Don't leave me! Let us die together! Oh, why did I come? Why did I come?" she wailed; while the other girl answered with a brave attempt at cheerfulness, as she put over Ethel's head the only life preserver she could find:

"I will! I will! Be calm, dear! I guess there is no immediate danger. Hold fast to this while I try to find something warm for you to put on."

In a moment Jenny's candle shone like a star of hope in the gloom, and by the time the three had got into wrappers and shawls, a peal of laughter from the Professor assured them that the danger could not be great. Other sounds of merriment, as well as Mrs. Sibley's voice scolding violently, were heard; and presently Mr. Homer came to tell them to be calm, for the stoppage was only to cool the engines, and the noise was occasioned by Joe Sibley's tumbling out of his berth in a fit of nightmare caused by Welsh rarebits and poached eggs at eleven at night.

Much relieved, and a little ashamed now of their fright, everyone subsided; but Ethel could not sleep, and clung to Jenny in an hysterical state till a soft voice began to sing "Abide with Me" so sweetly that more than one agitated listener blessed the singer and fell asleep before the comforting hymn ended.

Ethel was up next day, and lay on the Professor's bearskin rug on deck, looking pale and interesting, while the Sibleys sat by her talking over the exciting event of the night, to poor Joe's great disgust. Jenny crept to her usual corner, and sat with a book on her lap, quietly reviving in the fresh air till she was able to enjoy the pleasant chat of the Homers, who established themselves nearby and took care of her, learning each day to love and respect the faithful little soul who kept her worries to herself, and looked brightly forward no matter how black the sky might be.

Only one other incident of the voyage need be told; but as that marked a change in the relations between the two girls it is worth recording.

As she prepared for bed late one evening, Mrs. Homer heard Jenny say in a tone never used before:

"My dear, I must say something to you or I shall not feel as if I were doing my duty. I promised your mother that you should keep early hours, as you are not very strong and excitement is bad for you. Now, you *won't* come to bed at ten, as I ask you to every night, but stay up playing cards or sitting on deck till nearly everyone but the Sibleys is gone. Mrs. Homer waits for us, and is tired, and it is very rude to keep her up. Will you *please* do as you ought, and not oblige me to say you must?"

Ethel was sleepy and cross, and answered pettishly, as she held out her foot to have her boot unbuttoned, — for Jenny, anxious to please, refused no service asked of her:

"I shall do as I like, and you and Mrs. Homer needn't trouble yourselves about me. Mamma wished me to have a good time, and I shall! There is no harm in staying up to enjoy the moonlight, and sing and tell stories. Mrs. Sibley knows what is proper better than you do."

"I don't think she does, for she goes to bed and leaves the girls to flirt with those officers in a way that I know is *not* proper," answered Jenny firmly. "I should be very sorry to hear them say of you as they did of the Sibley girls, 'They are a wild lot, but great fun.' "

"Did they say that? How impertinent!" and Ethel bridled up like a ruffled chicken, for she was not out yet, and had not lost the modest instincts that so soon get blunted when a frivolous fashionable life begins.

"I heard them, and I know that the well-bred people on board do not like the Sibleys' noisy ways and bad manners. Now, you, my dear, are young and unused to this sort of life; so you cannot be too careful what you say and do, and with whom you go."

"Good gracious! anyone would think *you* were as wise as Solomon and as old as the hills. *You* are young, and *you* haven't traveled, and don't know any more of the world than I do — not so much of some things; so you needn't preach."

"I'm not wise nor old, but I *do* know more of the world than you, for I began to take care of myself and earn my living at sixteen, and four years of hard work have taught me a great deal. I am to watch over you, and I intend to do it faithfully, no matter what you say, nor how hard you make it for me; because I promised, and I shall keep my word. We are not to trouble Mrs. Homer with our little worries, but try to help each other and have a really good time. I will do anything for you that I can, but I shall *not* let you do things which I wouldn't allow my own sisters to do, and if you refuse to mind me, I shall write to your mother and ask to go home. My conscience won't let me take money and pleasure unless I earn them and do my duty."

"Well, upon my word!" cried Ethel, much impressed by such a decided speech from gentle Jane, and dismayed at the idea of being taken home in disgrace.

"We won't talk any more now, because we may get angry and say what we should be sorry for. I am sure you will see that I am right when you think it over quietly. So good-night, dear."

"Good-night," was all the reply Ethel gave, and a long silence followed.

Mrs. Homer could not help hearing as the staterooms were close together, and the well-ventilated doors made all conversation beyond a whisper audible.

"I didn't think Jane had the spirit to talk like that. She has taken my hint and asserted herself, and I'm very glad, for Ethel must be set right at once or we shall have no peace. She will respect and obey Jane after this, or I shall be obliged to say *my* word."

Mrs. Homer was right, and before her first nap set in she heard a meek voice say:

"Are you asleep, Miss Bassett?"

"No, dear."

"Then I want to say, I've thought it over. Please *don't* write to Mamma. I'll be good. I'm sorry I was rude to you; do forgive —"

The sentence was not ended, for a sudden rustle, a little sob, and several hearty kisses plainly told that Jenny had flown to pardon, comfort, and caress her naughty child, and that all was well.

After that Ethel's behavior was painfully decorous for the rest of the voyage, which, fortunately for her good resolutions, ended at Queenstown, much to her regret. The Homers thought a glimpse at Ireland and Scotland would be good for the girls; and as the Professor had business in Edinburgh this was the better route for all parties. But Ethel longed for London, and refused to see any beauty in the Lakes of Killarney, turned up her nose at jaunting-cars, and pronounced Dublin a stupid place.

Scotland suited her better, and she could not help enjoying the fine scenery with such companions as the Homers; for the Professor knew all about the relics and ruins, and his wife had a memory richly stored with the legends, poetry, and romance which make dull facts memorable and history enchanting.

But Jenny's quiet rapture was pleasant to behold. She had not scorned Scott's novels as old-fashioned, and she peopled the cottages and castles with his heroes and heroines; she crooned Burns's sweet songs to herself as she visited his haunts, and went about in a happy sort of dream, with her head full of Highland Mary, Tam o' Shanter, field mice and daisies, or fought terrific battles with Fitz-James and Marmion, and tried if "the light harebell" would "raise its head, elastic from her airy tread," as it did from the Lady of the Lake's famous foot.

Ethel told her she was "clean daft," but Jenny said, "Let me enjoy it while I can. I've dreamed of it so long I can hardly realize that it has come, and I cannot lose a minute of it." So she absorbed Scotch poetry and romance with the mist and the keen air from the moors, and bloomed like the bonnie heather which she loved to wear.

"What shall we do this rainy day in this stupid place?" said Ethel one morning, when bad weather kept them from an excursion to Stirling Castle.

"Write our journals and read up for the visit; then we shall know all about the castle, and need not tire people with our questions," answered Jenny, already established in a deep window-seat of their parlor at the hotel with her books and portfolio.

"I don't keep a journal, and I hate to read guide-books; it's much easier to ask, though there is very little I care for about these moldy old places," said Ethel with a yawn, as she looked out into the muddy street.

"How can you say so? Don't you care for poor Mary, and Prince Charlie, and all the other sad and romantic memories that haunt the country? Why, it seems as real to me as if it happened yesterday, and I never can forget anything about the place or the people now. Really, dear, I think you ought to take more interest and improve this fine chance. Just see how helpful and lovely Mrs. Homer is, with a quotation for every famous spot we see. It adds so much to our pleasure, and makes her so interesting. I'm going to learn some of the fine bits in this book of hers, and make them my own, since I cannot buy the beautiful little set this Burns belongs to. Don't you want to try it, and while away the dull day by hearing each other recite and talking over the beautiful places we have seen?"

"No, thank you; no study for me. It is to be all play now. Why tire my wits with that Scotch stuff when Mrs. Homer is here to do it for me?" and lazy Ethel turned to the papers on the table for amusement more to her taste.

"But we shouldn't think only of our own pleasure, you know. It is so sweet to be able to teach, amuse, or help others in any way. I'm glad to learn this new accomplishment, so that I may be to some one by and by what dear Mrs. Homer is to us now, if I ever can. Didn't you see how charmed those English people were at Holyrood when she was reciting those fine lines to us? The old gentleman bowed and thanked her, and the handsome lady called her 'a book of elegant extracts.' I thought it was such a pretty and pleasant thing that I described it all to mother and the girls."

"So it was; but did you know that the party was Lord Cumberland and his family? The guide told me afterward. I never guessed they were anybody, in such plain tweed gowns and thick boots; did you?"

"I knew they were ladies and gentlemen by their manners and conversation; did you expect they would travel in coronets and ermine mantles?" laughed Jenny.

"I'm not such a goose! But I'm glad we met them, because I can tell the Sibleys of it. They think so much of titles, and brag about Lady Watts Barclay, whose husband is only a brewer knighted. I shall buy a plaid like the one the lord's daughter wore, and wave it in the faces of those girls; they do put on *such* airs because they have been in Europe before."

Jenny was soon absorbed in her books; so Ethel curled herself up in the window-seat with an illustrated London paper full of some royal event, and silence reigned for an hour. Neither had seen the Professor's glasses rise like two full moons above his paper now and then to peep at them as they chatted at the other end of the room; neither saw him smile as he made a memorandum in his notebook, nor guessed how pleased he was at Jenny's girlish admiration of his plain but accomplished and excellent wife. It was one of the trifles which went to form his opinion of the two lasses, and in time to suggest a plan which ended in great joy for one of them.

"Now the real fun begins, and I shall be perfectly contented," cried Ethel as they rolled through the London streets towards the dingy Langham Hotel, where Americans love to congregate.

Jenny's eyes were sparkling also, and she looked as if quite ready for the new scenes and excitements which the famous old city promised them, though she had private doubts as to whether anything could be more delightful than Scotland.

The Sibleys were at the hotel; and the ladies of both parties at once began a round of shopping and sightseeing, while the gentlemen went about their more important affairs. Joe was detailed for escort duty; and a fine time the poor lad had of it, trailing about with seven ladies by day and packing them into two cabs at night for the theatres and concerts they insisted on trying to enjoy in spite of heat and weariness.

Mrs. Homer and Jenny were soon tired of this "whirl of gaiety," as they called it, and planned more quiet excursions, with some hours each day for rest and the writing and reading which all wise tourists make a part of their duty and pleasure. Ethel rebelled, and much preferred the "rabble," as Joe irreverently called his troop of ladies, never losing her delight in Regent Street shops, the parks at the fashionable hour, and the evening shows in full blast everywhere during the season. She left the sober party whenever she could escape, and with Mrs. Sibley as chaperone, frolicked about with the gay girls to her heart's content. It troubled Jenny, and made her feel as if she were not doing her duty; but Mrs. Homer consoled her by the fact that a month was all they could give to London, and soon the parties would separate, for the Sibleys were bound for Paris, and the Professor for Switzerland and Germany, through August and September.

So little Jane gave herself up to the pleasures she loved, and with the new friends, whose kindness she tried to repay by every small service in her power, spent happy days among the famous haunts they knew so well, learning much and storing away all she saw and heard for future profit and pleasure. A few samples of the different ways in which our young travelers improved their opportunities will sufficiently illustrate this new version of the gay grasshopper and the thrifty ant.

When they visited Westminster Abbey, Ethel was soon tired of tombs and chapels, and declared that the startling tableau of the skeleton Death peeping out of the half-opened door of the tomb to throw his dart at Mrs. Nightingale, and the ludicrous bas-relief of some great earl in full peer's robes and coronet being borne to heaven in the arms of fat cherubs puffing under their load, were the only things worth seeing.

Jenny sat spellbound in the Poets' Corner, listening while Mrs. Homer named the illustrious dead around them; followed the verger from chapel to chapel with intelligent interest as he told the story of each historical or royal tomb, and gave up Madam Tussaud's wax-work to spend several happy hours sketching the beautiful cloisters in the Abbey to add to her collection of water colors, taken as she went from place to place, to serve as studies for her pupils at home.

At the Tower she grew much excited over the tragic spots she visited and the heroic tales she heard of the kings and queens, the noble hearts and wise heads, that pined and perished there. Ethel "hated horrors," she said, and cared only for the crown jewels, the faded effigies in the armor gallery, and the queer Highlanders skirling on the bagpipes in the courtyard.

At Kew Jenny reveled in the rare flowers, and was stricken with amazement at the Victoria Regia, the royal water lily, so large that a child could sit on one of its vast leaves as on a green island. Her interest and delight so touched the heart of the crusty keeper that he gave her a nosegay of orchids, which excited the envy of Ethel and the Sibley girls, who were of the party, but had soon wearied of plants and gone off to order tea in Flora's Bower — one of the little cottages where visitors repose and refresh themselves with weak tea and Bath buns in such tiny rooms that they have to put their wraps in the fireplace or out of the window while they feast.

At the few parties to which they went — for the Homers'

friends were of the grave, elderly sort — Jenny sat in a corner taking notes of the gay scene, while Ethel yawned. But the Mouse got many a crumb of good conversation as she nestled close to Mrs. Homer, drinking in the wise and witty chat that went on between the friends who came to pay their respects to the Professor and his interesting wife. Each night Jenny had new and famous names to add to the list in her journal, and the artless pages were rich in anecdotes, descriptions, and comments on the day's adventures.

But the gem of her London collection of experiences was found in a most unexpected way, and not only gave her great pleasure, but made the young gadabouts regard her with sudden respect as one come to honor.

"Let me stay and wait upon you; I'd much rather than go to the Crystal Palace, for I shouldn't enjoy it at all with you lying here in pain and alone," said Jenny one lovely morning when the girls came down ready for the promised excursion, to find Mrs. Homer laid up with a nervous headache.

"No, dear, you can do nothing for me, thanks. Quiet is all I need, and my only worry is that I am not able to write up my husband's notes for him. I promised to have them ready last night, but was so tired I could not do it," answered Mrs. Homer, as Jenny leaned over her full of affectionate anxiety.

"Let me do them! I'd be so proud to help; and I can, for I did copy some one day, and he said it was well done. Please let me; I should enjoy a quiet morning here much better than the noisy party we shall have, since the Sibleys are to go."

With some reluctance the invalid consented; and when the rest were gone with hasty regrets, Jenny fell to work so briskly that in an hour or two the task was done. She was looking wistfully out of the window wondering where she could go alone, since Mrs. Homer was asleep and no one needed her, when the Professor came in to see how his wife was before he went to the British Museum to consult certain famous books and parchments.

He was much pleased to find his notes in order, and after a

glance at the sleeping lady, told Jenny she was to come with him for a visit to a place which *she* would enjoy, though most young people thought it rather dull.

Away they went; and being given in charge to a pleasant old man, Jenny roamed over the vast Museum where the wonders of the world are collected, enjoying every moment, till Mr. Homer called her away, as his day's work was done. It was late now, but she never thought of time, and came smiling up from the Egyptian Hall ready for the lunch the Professor proposed. They were just going out when a gentleman met them, and recognizing the American stopped to greet him cordially. Jenny's heart beat when she was presented to Mr. Gladstone, and she listened with all her ears to the silvery un-English voice, and stared with all her eyes at the weary yet wise and friendly face of the famous man.

"I'm so glad! I wanted to see him very much, and I feel so grand to think I've really had a bow and a smile all to myself from the Premier of England," said Jenny in a flutter of girlish delight when the brief interview was over.

"You shall go to the House of Commons with me and hear him speak some day; then your cup will be full, since you have already seen Browning, heard Irving, taken tea with Jean Ingelow, and caught a glimpse of the royal family," said the Professor, enjoying her keen interest in people and places.

"Oh, thanks! that will be splendid. I do love to see famous persons, because it gives me a true picture of them, and adds to my desire to know more of them, and admire their virtues or shun their faults."

"Yes, that sort of mental picture-gallery is a good thing to have, and we will add as many fine portraits as we can. Now you shall ride in a hansom, and see how you like that."

Jenny was glad to do so, for ladies do not use these vehicles when alone, and Ethel had put on great airs after a spin in one with Joe. Jenny was girl enough to like to have her little adventures to boast of, and that day she was to have another which eclipsed all that her young companions ever knew.

A brisk drive, a cozy lunch at a famous chop-house where Johnson had drunk oceans of tea, was followed by a stroll in the Park; for the Professor liked his young comrade, and was grateful for the well-written notes which helped on his work.

As they leaned against the railing to watch the splendid equipages roll by, one that seemed well known, though only conspicuous by its quiet elegance, stopped near them, and the elder of the two ladies in it bowed and beckoned to Professor Homer. He hastened forward to be kindly greeted and invited to drive along the Ladies' Mile. Jenny's breath was nearly taken away when she was presented to the Duchess of S———, and found herself sitting in a luxurious carriage opposite her Grace and her companion, with a white-wigged coachman perched aloft and two powdered footmen erect behind. Secretly rejoicing that she had made herself especially nice for her trip with the Professor, and remembering that young English girls are expected to efface themselves in the company of their elders, she sat mute and modest, stealing shy glances from under her hat-brim at the great lady, who was talking in the simplest way with her guest about his work, in which, as a member of one of the historical houses of England, she took much interest. A few gracious words fell to Jenny's share before they were set down at the door of the hotel, to the great admiration of the porter, who recognized the liveries and spread the news.

"This is a good sample of the way things go in Vanity Fair. We trudge away to our daily work afoot, we treat ourselves to a humble cab through the mud, pause in the park to watch the rich and great, get whisked into a ducal carriage, and come home in state, feeling rather exalted, don't we?" asked the Professor as they went upstairs, and he observed the new air of dignity which Jane unconsciously assumed as an obsequious waiter flew before to open the door.

"I think we do," answered honest Jane, laughing as she caught the twinkle of his eyes behind the spectacles. "I like splendor, and I am rather set up to think I've spoken to a live duchess; but I think I like her beautiful old face and charming manners more than her fine coach or great name. Why, she was much more simply dressed than Mrs. Sibley, and talked as pleasantly as if she did not feel a bit above us. Yet one couldn't forget that she was noble, and lived in a very different world from ours."

"That is just it, my dear; she *is* a noble woman in every sense of the word, and has a right to her title. Her ancestors were king-makers, and she is Lady-in-waiting to the Queen; yet she leads the charities of London, and is the friend of all who help the world along. I'm glad you have met her, and seen so good a sample of a true aristocrat. We Americans affect to scorn titles, but too many of us hanker for them in secret, and bow before very poor imitations of the real thing. Don't fill your journal with fine names, as some much wiser folk do, but set down only the best, and remember, 'All that glitters is not gold.' "

"I will, sir." And Jenny put away the little sermon side by side with the little adventure, saying nothing of either till Mrs. Homer spoke of it, having heard the story from her husband.

"How I wish I'd been there, instead of fagging round that great palace full of rubbish! A real Duchess! Won't the Sibleys stare? We shall hear no more of Lady Watts Barclay after this, I guess, and you will be treated with great respect; see if you are not!" said Ethel, much impressed with her companion's good fortune and eager to tell it.

"If things of that sort affect them, their respect is not worth having," answered Jane, quietly accepting the arm Ethel offered her as they went to dinner — a very unusual courtesy, the cause of which she understood and smiled at.

Ethel looked as if she felt the reproof, but said nothing, only set an example of greater civility to her companion, which the other girls involuntarily followed, after they had heard of Jenny's excursion with the Professor.

The change was very grateful to patient Jane, who had borne many small slights in proud silence; but it was soon over, for the parties separated, and our friends left the city far behind them, as they crossed the channel, and sailed up the Rhine to Schwalbach, where Mrs. Homer was to try the steel springs for her rheumatism while the Professor rested after his London labors.

A charming journey, and several very happy weeks followed as the girls roamed about the Little Brunnen, gay with people from all parts of Europe, come to try the famous mineral waters, and rest under the lindens.

Jenny found plenty to sketch here, and was busy all day booking picturesque groups as they sat in the Allée Saal, doing pretty woodland bits as they strolled among the hills, carefully copying the arches and statues in St. Elizabeth's Chapel, or the queer old houses in the Jews' Quarter of the town. Even the pigs went into the portfolio, with the little swineherd blowing his horn in the morning to summon each lazy porker from its sty to join the troop that trotted away to eat acorns in the oak wood on the hill till sunset called them home again.

Ethel's chief amusement was buying trinkets at the booths near the Stahlbrunnen. A tempting display of pretty crystal, agate, and steel jewelry was there, with French bonbons, Swiss carvings, German embroidery and lace-work, and most delectable little portfolios of views of fine scenery or illustrations of famous books. Ethel spent much money here, and added so greatly to her store of souvenirs that a new trunk was needed to hold the brittle treasures she accumulated in spite of the advice given her to wait till she reached Paris, where all could be bought much cheaper and packed safely for transportation.

Jenny contented herself with a German book, Kaulbach's Goethe Gallery, and a set of ornaments for each sister; the purple, pink, and white crystals being cheap and pretty trinkets for young girls. She felt very rich with her generous salary to draw upon when she liked; but having made a list of proper gifts, she resisted temptation and saved her money, remembering how much every penny was needed at home.

Driving from the ruins of Hohenstein one lovely afternoon, the girls got out to walk up a long hill, and amused themselves gathering flowers by the way. When they took their places again, Ethel had a great bouquet of scarlet poppies, Jenny a nosegay of blue cornflowers for Mrs. Homer, and a handful of green wheat for herself.

"You look as if you had been gleaning," said the Professor, as he watched the girls begin to trim their rough straw hats with the gay coquelicots and the bearded ears.

"I feel as if I were doing that every day, sir, and gathering in a great harvest of pleasure, if nothing else," answered Jenny, turning her bright eyes full of gratitude from one kind face to the other.

"My poppies are much prettier than that stiff stuff. Why didn't you get some?" asked Ethel, surveying her brilliant decoration with great satisfaction.

"They don't last; but my wheat will, and only grow prettier as it ripens in my hat," answered Jenny, contentedly settling the graceful spires in the straw cord that bound the pointed crown.

"Then the kernels will all drop out and leave the husks; that won't be nice, I'm sure," laughed Ethel.

"Well, some hungry bird will pick them up and be glad of them. The husks will last a long time and remind me of this happy day; your poppies are shedding their leaves already, and the odor is not pleasant. I like my honest bread-making wheat better than your opium flowers," said Jenny, with her thoughtful smile, as she watched the scarlet petals float away leaving the green seed-vessels bare.

"Oh, I shall get some artificial ones at my little milliner's, and be fine as long as I like; so you are welcome to your useful, bristly old wheat," said Ethel, rather nettled by the look that passed between the elders.

Nothing more was said; but both girls remembered that little talk long afterward, for those two wayside nosegays served to point the moral of this little tale, if not to adorn it.

We have no space to tell all the pleasant wanderings of our travelers as they went from one interesting place to another, till they paused for a good rest at Geneva.

Here Ethel quite lost her head among the glittering display of jewelry, and had to be watched lest she rashly spend her last penny. They were obliged almost forcibly to carry her out of the enchanting shops; and no one felt safe till she was either on the lake, or driving to Chamouni, or asleep in her bed.

Jenny bought a watch, a very necessary thing for a teacher, and this was the best place to get a good one. It was chosen with care and much serious consultation with the Professor; and Mrs. Homer added a little chain and seal, finding Jenny about to content herself with a black cord.

"It is only a return for many daughterly services, my dear; and my husband wishes me to offer these with thanks to the patient secretary who has often helped him so willingly," she said, as she came to wake Jenny with a kiss on the morning of her twenty-first birthday.

A set of little volumes like those she had admired was the second gift, and Jenny was much touched to be so kindly remembered. Ethel gave her some thread lace which she had longed to buy for her mother at Brussels, but did not, finding it as costly as beautiful. It was a very happy day, though quietly spent sitting by the lake enjoying the well-chosen extracts from Shakespeare, Wordsworth, Byron, Burns, Scott, and other descriptive poets, and writing loving letters home, proudly stamped with the little seal.

After that, while Ethel haunted the brilliant shops, read novels in the hotel garden, or listlessly followed the sightseers, Jenny, with the help of her valuable little library, her industrious pencil, and her accomplished guides, laid up a store of precious souvenirs as they visited the celebrated spots that lie like a necklace of pearls around the lovely lake, with Mont Blanc as the splendid opal that fitly clasps the chain. Calvin and Geneva, Voltaire and Ferney, De Staël and Coppet, Gibbon's garden at Lausanne, Byron's Prisoner at Chillon, Rousseau's chestnut grove at Clarens, and all the legends, relics, and memories of Switzerland's heroes, romancers, poets, and philosophers, were carefully studied, recorded, and enjoyed; and when at last they steamed away toward Paris, Jenny felt as if her head and her heart and one little trunk held richer treasures than all the jewelry in Geneva.

At Lyons her second important purchase was made; for when they visited one of the great manufactories to execute several commissions given to Mrs. Homer, Jenny proudly bought a nice black silk for her mother. This, with the delicate lace, would make the dear woman presentable for many a day, and the good girl beamed with satisfaction as she pictured the delight of all at home when this splendid gift appeared to adorn the dear parent-bird, who never cared how shabby she was if her young were well feathered.

It was a trial to Jenny, when they reached Paris, to spend day after day shopping, talking to dressmakers, and driving in the Bois to watch the elegant world on parade, when she longed to be living through the French Revolution with Carlyle, copying the quaint relics at Hôtel Cluny, or reveling in the treasures of the Louvre.

"Why *do* you want to study and poke all the time?" asked Ethel, as they followed Mrs. Homer and a French acquaintance round the Palais Royal one day with its brilliant shops, cafés, and crowds.

"My dream is to be able to take a place as teacher of German and history in a girl's school next year. It is a fine chance, and I am promised it if I am fitted; so I must work when I can to be ready.

That is why I like Versailles better than Rue de Rivoli, and enjoy talking with Professor Homer about French kings and queens more than I do buying mock diamonds and eating ices here," answered Jenny, looking very tired of the glitter, noise, and dust of the gay place when her heart was in the Conciergerie with poor Marie Antoinette, or the Invalides, where lay the great Napoleon still guarded by his faithful Frenchmen.

"What a dismal prospect! I should think you'd rather have a jolly time while you could, and trust to luck for a place by and by, if you must go on teaching," said Ethel, stopping to admire a window full of distracting bonnets.

"No; it is a charming prospect to me, for I love to teach, and I can't leave anything to luck. God helps those who help themselves, mother says, and I want to give the girls an easier time than I have had; so I shall get my tools ready, and fit myself to do good work when the job comes to me," answered Jenny, with such a decided air that the French lady glanced back at her, wondering if a quarrel was going on between the demoiselles.

"What do you mean by tools?" asked Ethel, turning from the gay bonnets to a ravishing display of bonbons in the next window.

"Professor Homer said one day that a well-stored mind was a tool chest with which one could carve one's way. Now, my tools are knowledge, memory, taste, the power of imparting what I know, good manners, sense, and — patience," added Jenny with a sigh, as she thought of the weary years spent in teaching little children the alphabet.

Ethel took the sigh to herself, well knowing that she had been a trial, especially of late, when she had insisted on Jane's company because her own French was so imperfect as to be nearly useless, though at home she had flattered herself that she knew a good deal. Her own ignorance of many things had been unpleasantly impressed upon her lately, for at Madame Dene's Pension there were several agreeable English and French ladies, and much interesting conversation went on at the table, which Jenny heartily enjoyed, though she modestly said very little. But Ethel, longing to distinguish herself before the quiet English girls, tried to talk and often made sad mistakes because her head was a jumble of new names and places, and her knowledge of all kinds very superficial. Only the day before she had said in a patronizing tone to a French lady: —

"Of course we remember our obligations to your Lamartine during our Revolution, and the other brave Frenchmen who helped us."

"You mean Lafayette, dear," whispered Jenny quickly, as the lady smiled and bowed, bewildered by the queerly pronounced French, but catching the poet's name.

"I know what I mean; you needn't trouble yourself to correct and interrupt me when I'm talking," answered Ethel in her pert way, annoyed by a smile on the face of the girl opposite, and Jenny's blush at her rudeness and ingratitude. She regretted both when Jane explained the matter afterward, and wished that she had at once corrected what would then have passed as a slip of the tongue. Now it was too late; but she kept quiet and gave Miss Cholmondeley no more chances to smile in that aggravatingly superior way, though it was very natural, as she was a highly educated girl.

Thinking of this, and many other mistakes of her own from which Jane tried to save her, Ethel felt a real remorse, and walked silently on, wondering how she could reward this kind creature who had served her so well and was so anxious to get on in her hard, humble way. The orders were all given now, the shopping nearly done, and Mademoiselle Campan, the elderly French lady who boarded at their Pension, was always ready to jaunt about and be useful; so why not give Jane a holiday, and let her grub and study for the little while left them in Paris? In a fortnight Uncle Sam was to pick up the girls and take them home, while the Homers went to Rome for the winter. It would be well to take Miss Bassett back in a good humor, so that her report would please Mamma, and appease Papa if he were angry at the amount of money spent by his extravagant little daughter. Ethel saw now, as one always does when it is too late to repair damages, many things left undone which she ought to have done, and regretted living for herself instead of putting more pleasure into the life of this good girl, whose future seemed so uninviting to our young lady with her first season very near.

It was a kind plan, and gratified Jenny very much when it was proposed and proved to her that no duty would be neglected if she went about with the Homers and left her charge to the excellent lady who enjoyed *chiffons* as much as Ethel did, and was glad to receive pretty gifts in return for her services.

But alas for Ethel's good resolutions and Jenny's well-earned holiday! Both came to nothing, for Ethel fell ill from too much pastry, and had a sharp bilious attack which laid her up till the uncle arrived.

Everyone was very kind, and there was no danger; but the days were long, the invalid very fretful, and the nurse very tired, before the second week brought convalescence and a general cheering and clearing-up took place. Uncle Sam was amusing himself very comfortably while he waited for his niece to be able to travel, and the girls were beginning to pack by degrees, for the accumulation of Ethel's purchases made her share a serious task.

"There! All are in now, and only the steamer trunk is left to pack at the last moment," said Jenny, folding her tired arms after a protracted struggle with half a dozen new gowns and a perplexing medley of hats, boots, gloves, and perfumery. Two large trunks stood in the anteroom ready to go; the third was now done, and nothing remained but the small one and Jenny's shabby portmanteau.

"How nicely you have managed! I ought to have helped, only you wouldn't let me and I should have spoiled my wrapper. Come and rest and help me sort out this rubbish," said Ethel, who would have been dressed and out if the arrival of a new *peignoir* had not kept her in to enjoy the lovely pink-and-blue thing, all lace and ribbon and French taste.

"You will never get them into that box, dear," answered Jenny, gladly sitting down beside her on the sofa, which was strewn with trinkets of all sorts, more or less damaged by careless handling, and the vicissitudes of a wandering trunk.

"I don't believe they are worth fussing over. I'm tired of them, and they look very mean and silly after seeing real jewels here. I'd throw them away if I hadn't spent so much money on them," said Ethel, turning over the tarnished filigree, mock pearl, and imitation coral necklaces, bracelets, and brooches that were tumbling out of the frail boxes in which they came.

"They will look pretty to people at home who have not been seeing so many as we have. I'll sew up the broken cases, and rub up the silver, and string the beads, and make all as good as new, and you will find plenty of girls at home glad to get them, I am sure," answered Jenny, rapidly bringing order out of chaos with those skillful hands of hers.

Ethel leaned back and watched her silently for a few minutes. During this last week our young lady had been thinking a good deal, and was conscious of a strong desire to tell Jane Bassett how much she loved and thanked her for all her patient and faithful care during the six months now nearly over. But she was proud, and humility was hard to learn; self-will was sweet, and to own one's self in the wrong a most distasteful task. The penitent did not know how to begin, so waited for an opportunity, and presently it came.

"Shall you be glad to get home, Jenny?" she asked in her most caressing tone, as she hung her prettiest locket round her friend's neck; for during this illness all formality and coolness had melted away, and "Miss Bassett" was "Jenny dear" now.

"I shall be very, very glad to see my precious people again, and tell them all about my splendid holiday; but I can't help wishing that we were to stay till spring, now that we are here, and I have no teaching, and may never get such another chance. I'm afraid it seems ungrateful when I've had so much; but to go back without seeing Rome is a trial, I confess," answered honest Jane, rubbing away at a very dull paste bandeau.

"So it is; but I don't mind so much, because I shall come again by and by, and I mean to be better prepared to enjoy things properly than I am now. I'll really study this winter, and not be such a fool. Jenny, I've a plan in my head. I wonder if you'd like it? I should immensely, and I'm going to propose it to Mamma the minute I get home," said Ethel, glad to seize this opening.

"What is it, dearie?"

"Would you like to be my governess and teach me all you know, quietly, at home this winter? I don't want to begin school again just for languages and a few finishing things, and I really think you would do more for me than anyone else, because you know what I need, and are so patient with your bad, ungrateful, saucy girl. Could you? Would you come?" and Ethel put her arms round Jenny's neck with a little sob and a kiss that was far more precious to Jane than the famous diamond necklace of Marie Antoinette, which she had been reading about.

"I could and I would with all my heart, if you want me, darling! I think we know and love each other now; and can be happy and helpful together, and I'll come so gladly if your mother asks me," answered Jenny, quick to understand what underlay this sudden tenderness, and glad to accept the atonement offered her for many trials which she would never have told even to her own mother.

Ethel was her best self now, and her friend felt well rewarded for the past by this promise of real love and mutual help in the future. So they talked over the new plan in great spirits till Mrs. Homer came to bring them their share of a packet of home letters just arrived. She saw that something unusual was going on, but only smiled, nodded, and went away saying:

"I have good news in *my* letters, and hope yours will make you equally happy, girls."

Silence reigned for a time, as they sat reading busily; then a sudden exclamation from Ethel seemed to produce a strange effect upon Jenny, for with a cry of joy she sprang up and danced all over the room, waving her letter wildly as she cried out:

"I'm to go! I'm to go! I can't believe it — but here it is! How kind, how very kind everyone is to me!" and down she went upon her own little bed to hide her face and laugh and cry till Ethel ran to rejoice with her.

"Oh, Jenny, I'm so glad! You deserve it, and it's like Mrs. Homer to make all smooth before she said a word. Let me read what Mamma writes to you. Here's my letter; see how sweetly she speaks of you, and how grateful they are for all you've done for me."

The letters changed hands; and sitting side by side in an affectionate bunch, the girls read the happy news that granted the cherished wish of one and gave the other real unselfish pleasure in another's happiness.

Jane was to go to Rome with the Homers for the winter, and perhaps to Greece in the spring. A year of delight lay before her, offered in such a friendly way, and with such words of commendation, thanks, and welcome, that the girl's heart was full, and she felt that every small sacrifice of feeling, every lonely hour, and distasteful duty was richly repaid by this rare opportunity to enjoy still further draughts of the wisdom, beauty, and poetry of the wonderful world now open to her.

She flew off presently to try to thank her good friends, and came back dragging a light new trunk, in which she nearly buried her small self as she excitedly explained its appearance, while rattling out the trays and displaying its many conveniences.

"That dear woman says I'm to send my presents home in the old one by you, and take this to fill up in Rome. Think of it! A lovely new French trunk, and Rome full of pictures, statues, St. Peter's, and the Colosseum. It takes my breath away and makes my head spin."

"So I see. It's a capital box, but it won't hold even St. Peter's, dear; so you'd better calm down and pack your treasures. I'll help," cried Ethel, sweeping about in her gay gown, almost as wild as Jane, who was quite upset by this sudden delicious change in her prospects.

How happily she laid away in the old trunk the few gifts she had ventured to buy, and those given her — the glossy silk, the dainty lace, the pretty crystals, the store of gloves, the flask of cologne, the pictures and books, and last of all the sketches which illustrated the journal kept so carefully for those at home.

"Now, when my letter is written and the check with all that is left of my salary put in, I am done. There's room for more, and I wish I'd got something else, now I feel so rich. But it is foolish to buy gowns to pay duties on, when I don't know what the girls need. I feel so rich now, I shall fly out and pick up some more little pretties for the dears. They have so few, anything will be charming to them," said Jenny, proudly surveying her box, and looking about for some foreign trifle with which to fill up the corners.

"Then let me put these in, and so be rid of them. I shall go to see your people and tell them all about you, and explain how you came to send so much rubbish."

As she spoke Ethel slipped in several Swiss carvings, the best of the trinkets, and a parcel of dainty Parisian ties and sashes which would gladden the hearts of the poor, pretty girls, just beginning to need such aids to their modest toilets. A big box of bonbons completed her contribution, and left but one empty corner.

"I'll tuck in my old hat to keep all steady; the girls will like it when they dress up, and I'm fond of it, because it recalls some of my happiest days," said Jenny, as she took up the well-worn hat and began to dust it. A shower of grain dropped into her hand, for the yellow wheat still kept its place and recalled the chat at Schwalbach. Ethel glanced at her own hat with its faded artificial flowers; and as her eye went from the small store of treasures so carefully and happily gathered to the strew of almost useless finery on her bed, she said soberly:

"You were right, Jenny. My poppies are worthless, and my harvest a very poor one. Your wheat fell in good ground, and you will glean a whole stack before you go home. Well, I shall keep *my* old hat to remind me of you; and when I come again, I hope I shall have a wiser head to put into a new one."

KATE'S CHOICE

from *Aunt Jo's Scrap Bag*
(Volume III), 1872

It is very plain in all of her work how much Louisa Alcott loved people, of all sorts and kinds. But she was often impatient with the formal society of her time, with its competitiveness and artificial manners and customs. Her belief in the value of simple living, which certain difficulties in her own life made clear to her, is voiced in her books and stories again and again, and is truly represented here in the account of Kate's Choice.

KATE'S CHOICE

"Well, what do you think of her?"

"I think she's a perfect dear, and not a bit stuck up with all her money."

"A real little lady, and ever so pretty."

"She kissed me lots, and doesn't tell me to run away, so I love her."

The group of brothers and sisters standing round the fire laughed as little May finished the chorus of praise with these crowning virtues.

Tall Alf asked the question, and seemed satisfied with the general approval of the new cousin just come from England to live with them. They had often heard of Kate, and rather prided themselves on the fact that she lived in a fine house, was very rich, and sent them charming presents. Now pity was added to the pride, for Kate was an orphan, and all her money could not buy back the parents she had lost. They had watched impatiently for her arrival, had welcomed her cordially, and after a day spent in trying to make her feel at home they were comparing notes in the twilight, while Kate was having a quiet talk with Mamma.

"I hope she will choose to live with us. You know she can go to any of the uncles she likes best," said Alf.

"We are nearer her age than any of the other cousins, and Papa is the oldest uncle, so I guess she will," added Milly, the fourteen-year-old daughter of the house.

"She said she liked America," said quiet Frank.

"Wonder if she will give us a lot of her money?" put in practical Fred, who was always in debt.

"Stop that!" commanded Alf. "Mind now, if you ever ask her for a penny I'll shake you out of your jacket."

"Hush! She's coming," cried Milly, and a dead silence followed the lively chatter.

A fresh-faced bright-eyed girl of fifteen came quietly in, glanced at the group on the rug, and paused as if doubtful whether she was wanted.

"Come on!" said Fred, encouragingly.

"Shall I be in the way?"

"Oh! Dear, no, we were only talking," answered Milly, drawing her cousin nearer with an arm about her waist.

"It sounded like something pleasant," said Kate, not exactly knowing what to say.

"We were talking about you," began little May, when a poke from Frank made her stop to ask, "What's that for? We *were* talking about Kate, and we all said we liked her, so it's no matter if I do tell."

"You are very kind," and Kate looked so pleased that the children forgave May's awkward frankness.

"Yes, and we hoped you'd like us and stay with us," said Alf, in the lofty and polite manner which he thought became the young lord of the house.

"I am going to try all the uncles in turn, and then decide; Papa wished it," answered Kate, with a sudden tremble of the lips, for her father was the only parent she could remember, and had been unusually dear for that reason.

"Can you play billiards?" asked Fred, who had a horror of seeing girls cry.

"Yes, and I'll teach you."

"You had a pony-carriage at your house, didn't you?" added Frank, eager to help on the good work.

"At Grandma's — I had no other home, you know," answered Kate.

"What shall you buy first with your money?" asked May, who *would* ask improper questions.

"I'd buy a grandma if I could," and Kate both smiled and sighed.

"How funny! We've got one somewhere, but we don't care much about her," continued May, with the inconvenient candor of a child.

"Have you? Where is she?" and Kate turned quickly, looking full of interest.

"Papa's mother is very old, and lives ever so far away in the country, so of course we don't see much of her," explained Alf.

"But Papa writes sometimes, and Mamma sends her things every Christmas. We don't remember her much, because we never saw her but once, ever so long ago; but we do care for her, and May mustn't say such rude things," said Milly.

"I shall go and see her. I can't get on without a grandmother," and Kate smiled so brightly that the lads thought her prettier than ever. "Tell me more about her. Is she a dear old lady?"

"Don't know. She is lame, and lives in the old house, and has a maid named Dolly, and — that's all I can tell you about her," and Milly looked a little vexed that she could say no more on the subject that seemed to interest her cousin so much.

Kate looked surprised, but said nothing, and stood looking at the fire as if turning the matter over in her mind, and trying to answer the question she was too polite to ask — how could they live without a grandmother? Here the tea-bell rang, and the flock ran laughing downstairs; but, though she said no more, Kate remembered that conversation, and laid a plan in her resolute little mind which she carried out when the time came.

According to her father's wish she lived for a while in the family of each of the four uncles before she decided with which she would make her home. All were anxious to have her, one because of her money, another because her great-grandfather had been a lord, a third hoped to secure her for his son, while the fourth and best family loved her for herself alone. They were worthy people, as the world goes — busy, ambitious, and prosperous; and every-one, old and young, was fond of bright, pretty, generous Kate. Each family was anxious to keep her, a little jealous of the rest, and very eager to know which she would choose.

But Kate surprised them all by saying decidedly when the time came:

"I must see Grandma before I choose. Perhaps I ought to have visited her first, as she is the oldest. I think Papa would wish me to do it. At any rate, I want to pay my duty to her before I settle anywhere, so please let me go."

Some of the young cousins laughed at the idea, and her old-fashioned, respectful way of putting it, which contrasted strongly with their free-and-easy American speech. The uncles were sur-prised, but agreed to humor her whim, and Uncle George, the eld-est, said softly:

"I ought to have remembered that poor Anna was Mother's only daughter, and the old lady would naturally love to see the girl. But, my dear, it will be desperately dull. Only two old women and a quiet country town. No fun, no company, you won't stay long."

"I shall not mind the dullness if Grandma likes to have me there. I lived very quietly in England, and was never tired of it. Nursey can take care of me, and I think the sight of me will do the dear old lady good, because they tell me I am like Mamma."

Something in the earnest young face reminded Uncle George of the sister he had almost forgotten, and recalled his own youth so pleasantly that he said, with a caress of the curly head beside him:

"So it would, I'm sure of it, and I've a great mind to go with you and 'pay my duty' to Mother, as you prettily express it."

"Oh, no, please don't, sir; I want to surprise her, and have her all to myself for a little while. Would you mind if I went quite alone with Nursey? You can come later."

"Not a bit; you shall do as you like, and make sunshine for the old lady as you have for us. I haven't seen her for a year, but I know she is well and comfortable, and Dolly guards her like a dragon. Give her my love, Kitty, and tell her I send her something she will value a hundred times more than the very best tea, the finest cap, or the handsomest tabby that ever purred."

So, in spite of the lamentations of her cousins, Kate went gaily away to find the Grandma whom no one else seemed to value as she did.

You see, Grandpa had been a farmer, and lived contentedly on the old place until he died; but his four sons wanted to be something better, so they went away one after the other to make their way in the world. All worked hard, got rich, lived splendidly, and forgot as far as possible the old life and the dull old place they came from. They were good sons in their way, and had each offered his mother a home with him if she cared to come. But Grandma clung to the old home, the simple ways, and quiet life, and, thanking them gratefully, she had remained in the big farmhouse, empty, lonely, and plain though it was, compared to the fine homes of her sons.

Little by little the busy men forgot the quiet, uncomplaining old mother, who spent her years thinking of them, longing to see and know their children, hoping they would one day remember how she loved them all, and how solitary her life must be.

Now and then they wrote or paid her a hasty visit, and all sent gifts of far less value to her than one loving look, one hour of dutiful, affectionate companionship.

"If you ever want me, send and I'll come. Or, if you ever need a home, remember the old place is here always open, and you are always welcome," the good old lady said. But they never seemed to need her, and so seldom came that the old place evidently had no charm for them.

It was hard, but the sweet old woman bore it patiently, and lived her lonely life quietly and usefully, with her faithful maid Dolly to serve and love and support her.

Kate's mother, her one daughter, had married young, gone to England, and, dying early, had left the child to its father and his family. Among them little Kate had grown up, knowing scarcely anything of her American relations until she was left an orphan and went back to her mother's people. She had been the pet of her English grandmother, and, finding all the aunts busy, fashionable women, had longed for the tender fostering she had known, and now felt as if only grandmothers could give.

With a flutter of hope and expectation she approached the old house after the long journey was over. Leaving the luggage at the inn, and accompanied by faithful Nurse, Kate went up the village street, and, pausing at the gate, looked at the home where her mother had been born.

A large, old-fashioned farmhouse, with a hospitable porch and tall trees in front, an orchard behind, and a capital hill for black-berries in summer, and coasting in winter, close by. All the upper windows were curtained, and made the house look as if it was half asleep. At one of the lower windows sat a portly puss, blinking in the sun, and at the other appeared a cap, a regular grandmotherly old cap, with a little black bow perked up behind. Something in the lonely look of the house and the pensive droop of that cap made Katy hurry up the walk and tap eagerly at the antique knocker. A brisk little old woman peered out, as if startled at the sound, and Kate asked, smiling, "Does Madam Coverley live here?"

"She does, dear. Walk right in," and throwing wide the door, the maid trotted down a long, wide hall, and announced in a low tone to her mistress:

"A nice, pretty little girl wants to see you, mum."

"I shall love to see a young face. Who is it, Dolly?" asked a pleasant voice.

"Don't know, mum."

"Grandma must guess," and Kate went straight up to the old lady with both hands out, for the first sight of that sweet old face won her heart.

Lifting her spectacles, Grandma looked silently a minute, then opened her arms without a word, and in the long embrace that followed Kate felt assured that she was welcome to the home she wanted.

"So like my Anna! And this is her little girl? God bless you, my darling! So good to come and see me!" said the old lady when she could speak.

"Why, Grandma, I couldn't get on without you, and as soon as I knew where to find you I was in a fidget to be off; but had to do my other visits first, because the uncles had planned it so. This is Dolly, I am sure, and that is my good nurse. Go and get my things, please, Nursey. I shall stay here until Grandma sends me away."

"That will never be, dearie. Now tell me everything. It is like an angel coming to see me all of a sudden. Sit close, and let me feel sure it isn't one of the dreams I make to cheer myself when I'm lonesome."

Kate sat on a little stool at Grandma's feet, and, leaning on her knee, told all her little story, while the old lady fed her hungry eyes with the sight of the fresh young face, listened to the music of a loving voice, and felt the happy certainty that someone had remembered her, as she longed to be remembered.

Such a happy day as Kate spent talking and listening, looking at her new home, which she found delightful, and being petted by the two old women, who would hardly let Nursey do anything for her. Kate's quick eyes read the truth of Grandma's lonely life very soon; her warm heart was full of tender pity, and she resolved to devote herself to making the happiness of the dear old lady's few remaining years, for at eighty one should have the prop of loving children, if ever.

To Dolly and madam it really did seem as if an angel had come, a singing, smiling, chattering sprite, who danced all over the old house, making blithe echoes in the silent rooms, and brightening every corner she entered.

Kate opened all the shutters and let in the sun, saying she must see which room she liked best before she settled. She played on the old piano, that wheezed and jangled, all out of tune; but no one minded, for the girlish voice was as sweet as a lark's. She invaded Dolly's sacred kitchen, and messed to her heart's content, delighting the old soul by praises of her skill, and petitions to be taught all she knew. She pranced to and fro in the long hall, and got acquainted with the lives of painted ancestors hanging there in big wigs or short-waisted gowns. She took possession of Grandma's little parlor, and made it so cozy the old lady felt as if she was bewitched, for cushioned armchairs, fur footstools, soft rugs, and delicate warm shawls appeared like magic. Flowers bloomed in the deep, sunny window-seats, pictures of lovely places seemed to break out on the oaken walls, a dainty work-basket took its place near Grandma's quaint one, and, best of all, the little chair beside her own was seldom empty now.

The first thing in the morning a kiss waked her, and the beloved voice gave her a gay "Good morning, Grandma dear!" All day Anna's child hovered about her with willing hands and feet to serve her, loving heart to return her love, and the tender reverence which is the beautiful tribute the young should pay the old. In the twilight, the bright head always was at her knees; and, in either listening to the stories of the past or making lively plans for the future, Kate whiled away the time that used to be so sad.

Kate never found it lonely, seldom wished for other society, and grew every day more certain that here she could find the cherishing she needed, and do the good she hoped.

Dolly and Nurse got on capitally; each tried which could sing "Little Missy's" praises loudest, and spoil her quickest by unquestioning obedience to every whim or wish. A happy family, and the dull November days went by so fast that Christmas was at hand before they knew it.

All the uncles had written to ask Kate to pass the holidays with them, feeling sure she must be longing for a change. But she had refused them all, saying she should stay with Grandma, who could not go anywhere to join other people's merrymakings, and must have one of her own at home. The uncles urged, the aunts advised, and the cousins teased; but Kate denied them all, yet offended no one, for she was inspired by a grand idea, and carried it out with help from Dolly and Nurse, unsuspected by Grandma.

"We are going to have a little Christmas fun up here among ourselves, and you mustn't know about it until we are ready. So just sit all cozy in your corner, and let me riot about as I like. I know you won't mind, and I think you'll say it is splendid when I've carried out my plan," said Kate, when the old lady wondered what she was thinking about so deeply, with her brows knit and her lips smiling.

"Very well, dear, do anything you like, and I shall enjoy it, only don't get tired, or try to do too much," and with that Grandma became deaf and blind to the mysteries that went on about her.

She was lame, and seldom left her own rooms; so Kate, with her devoted helpers, turned the house topsy-turvy, trimmed up hall and parlors and great dining room with shining holly and ever-green, laid fires ready for kindling on the hearths that had been cold for years, and had beds made up all over the house.

What went on in the kitchen, only Dolly could tell; but such delicious odors as stole out made Grandma sniff the air, and think of merry Christmas revels long ago. Up in her own room Kate wrote lots of letters, and sent orders to the city that made Nursey hold up her hands. More letters came in reply, and Kate had a rapture over every one. Big bundles were left by the express, who came so often that the gates were opened and the lawn soon full of sleigh tracks. The shops in the village were ravaged by Mistress

Kate, who laid in stores of gay ribbons, toys, nuts, and all manner of queer things.

"I really think she's lost her mind," said the postmaster as she flew out of the office one day with a handful of letters.

"Pretty creter! I wouldn't say a word against her, not for a mint of money. She's so good to old Mrs. Coverley," answered his fat wife, smiling as she watched Kate ride up the village street on an ox-sled.

If Grandma had thought the girl out of her wits, no one could have blamed her, for on Christmas day she really did behave in the most singular manner.

"You are going to church with me this morning, Grandma. It's all arranged. A closed carriage is coming for us, the sleighing is lovely, the church all trimmed up, and I must have you see it. I shall wrap you in fur, and we will go and say our prayers together, like good girls, won't we?" said Kate, who was in a queer flutter, while her eyes shone, her lips were all smiles, and her feet kept dancing in spite of her.

"Anywhere you like, my darling. I'd start for Australia tomorrow, if you wanted me to go with you," answered Grandma, who obeyed Kate in all things, and seemed to think she could do no wrong.

So they went to church, and Grandma did enjoy it; for she had many blessings to thank God for, chief among them the treasure of a dutiful, loving child. Kate tried to keep herself quiet, but the odd little flutter would not subside, and seemed to get worse and worse as time went on. It increased rapidly as they drove home, and, when Grandma was safe in her little parlor again, Kate's hands trembled so she could hardly tie the strings of the old lady's state and festival cap.

"We must take a look at the big parlor. It is all trimmed up, and I've got my presents in there. Is it ready, Doll?" asked Kate, as the old servant appeared, looking so excited that Grandma said, laughing:

"We have been quiet so long, poor Dolly don't know what to make of a little gaiety."

"Lord bless us, my dear mum! It's all so beautiful and kinder surprisin', I feel as ef merrycles had come to pass agin," answered Dolly, actually wiping away tears with her best white apron.

"Come, Grandma," and Kate offered her arm. "Don't she look sweet and dear?" she added, smoothing the soft, silken shawl about the old lady's shoulders, and kissing the placid old face that beamed at her from under the new cap.

"I always said madam was the finest old lady a-goin', ef folks only knew it. Now, Missy, ef you don't make haste, that parlor door will bust open, and spoil the surprise; for they are just bilin' over in there," with which mysterious remark Dolly vanished, giggling.

Across the hall they went, but at the door Kate paused, and said with a look Grandma never forgot:

"I hope I have done right. I hope you'll like my present, and not find it too much for you. At any rate, remember I meant to please you and give you the thing you need and long for most, my dear old Grandma."

"My good child, don't be afraid. I shall like anything you do, and thank you for your thought of me. What a curious noise! I hope the fire hasn't fallen down."

Without another word, Kate threw open the door and led Grandma in. Only a step or two — for the old lady stopped short and stared about her, as if she didn't know her own best parlor. No wonder she didn't, for it was full of people, and such people! All her sons, their wives and children, rose as she came in, and turned to greet her with smiling faces. Uncle George went up and kissed her, saying, with a choke in his voice, "A merry Christmas, Mother!" and everybody echoed the words in a chorus of goodwill that went straight to the heart.

Poor Grandma could not bear it, and sat down in her big chair, trembling, and sobbing like a little child. Kate hung over her, fearing the surprise had been too much; but joy seldom kills, and presently the old lady was calm enough to look up and welcome them all by stretching out her feeble hands and saying, brokenly yet heartily:

"God bless you, my children! This *is* a merry Christmas, indeed! Now tell me all about it, and who everybody is; for I don't know half the little ones."

Then Uncle George explained that it was Kate's plan, and told how she had made everyone agree to it, pleading so eloquently for Grandma that all other plans were given up. They had arrived while she was at church, and had been with difficulty kept from bursting out before the time.

"Do you like your present?" whispered Kate, quite calm and happy now that the grand surprise was safely over.

Grandma answered with a silent kiss that said more than the warmest words, and then Kate put everyone at ease by leading up the children, one by one, and introducing each with some lively speech. Everybody enjoyed this and got acquainted quickly; for Grandma thought the children the most remarkable she had ever seen, and the little people soon made up their minds that an old lady who had such a very nice, big house, and such a dinner waiting for them (of course they had peeped everywhere), was a most desirable and charming Grandma.

By the time the first raptures were over, Dolly and Nurse and Betsey Jane (a girl hired for the occasion) had got dinner on the table; and the procession, headed by Madam proudly escorted by her eldest son, filed into the dining room where such a party had not met for years.

It would be quite impossible to do justice to that dinner: pen and ink are not equal to it. I can only say that everyone partook copiously of everything; that they laughed and talked, told stories, and sang songs; and when no one could do any more, Uncle George proposed Grandma's health, which was drunk standing, and followed by three cheers. Then up got the old lady, quite rosy and young, excited and gay, and said in a clear strong voice —

"I give you in return the best of grandchildren, little Kate."

I give you my word the cheer they gave Grandma was nothing to the shout that followed these words; for the old lady led off with amazing vigor, and the boys roared so tremendously that the sedate tabby in the kitchen flew off her cushion, nearly frightened into a fit.

After that, the elders sat with Grandma in the parlor, while the younger part of the flock trooped after Kate all over the house. Fires burned everywhere, and the long unused toys of their fathers were brought out for their amusement. The big nursery was full of games, and here Nursey collected the little ones when the larger boys and girls were invited by Kate to go out and coast. Sleds had been provided, and until dusk they kept it up, the city girls getting as gay and rosy as Kate herself in this healthy sport, while the lads frolicked to their hearts' content, building snow forts, pelting one another, and carousing generally without any policeman to interfere or any stupid old ladies to get upset, as at home in the park.

A cozy tea and a dance in the long hall followed, and they were just thinking what they would do next, when Kate's second surprise came.

There were two great fireplaces in the hall: up the chimney of one roared a jolly fire, but the other was closed by a tall fire-board. As they sat about, resting after a brisk contra dance, a queer rustling and tapping was heard behind this fire-board.

"Rats!" suggested the girls, jumping up into the chairs.

"Let's have 'em out!" added the boys, making straight for the spot, intent on fun.

But before they got there, a muffled voice cried, "Stand from under!" and down went the board with a crash, out bounced Santa Claus, startling the lads as much as the rumor of rats had the girls.

A jolly old saint he was, all in fur, with sleigh-bells jingling from his waist and the point of his high cap, big boots, a white beard, and a nose as red as if Jack Frost had had a good tweak at it. Giving himself a shake that set all the bells ringing, he stepped out upon the hearth, saying in a half-gruff, half-merry tone:

"I call this a most inhospitable way to receive me! What do you mean by stopping up my favorite chimney? Never mind, I'll forgive you, for this is an unusual occasion. Here, some of you fellows, lend a hand and help me out with my sack."

A dozen pair of hands had the great bag out in a minute, and, lugging it to the middle of the hall, left it beside St. Nick, while the boys fell back into the eager, laughing crowd that surrounded the newcomer.

"Where's my girl? I want my Kate," said the saint, and when she went to him he took a base advantage of his years, and kissed her in spite of the beard.

"That's not fair," whispered Kate, as rosy as the holly berries in her hair.

"Can't help it — must have some reward for sticking in that horrid chimney so long," answered Santa Claus, looking as roguish as any boy. Then he added aloud, "I've got something for everybody, so make a big ring, and the good fairy will hand round the gifts."

With that he dived into his bag and brought out treasure after treasure, some fine, some funny, many useful, and all appropriate, for the good fairy seemed to have guessed what each one wanted. Shouts of laughter greeted the droll remarks of the jolly saint, for he had a joke about everything, and people were quite exhausted by the time the bottom of the sack was reached.

"Now, then, a rousing good game of blind man's buff, and then this little family must go to bed, for it's past eleven."

As he spoke, the saint cast off his cap and beard, fur coat, and big boots, and proceeded to dance a double shuffle with great vigor and skill; while the little ones, who had been thoroughly mystified, shouted, "Why, it's Alf!" and fell upon him *en masse* as the best way of expressing their delight at his successful performance of that immortal part.

The game of blind man's buff that followed was a "rouser" in every sense of the word, for the gentlemen joined, and the children flew about like a flock of chickens when hawks are abroad. Such peals of laughter, such shouts of fun, and such racing and scrambling that old hall had never seen before. Kate was so hunted that she finally took refuge behind Grandma's chair, and stood there looking at the lively scene, her face full of happiness as she remembered that it was her work.

The going to bed that night was the best joke of all; for, though Kate's arrangements were peculiar, everyone voted that they were capital. There were many rooms, but not enough for all to have one apiece. So the uncles and aunts had the four big chambers, all the boys were ordered into the great playroom, where beds were made on the floor, and a great fire blazing that the camping out might be as comfortable as possible. The nursery was devoted to the girls, and the little ones were sprinkled round wherever a snug corner was found.

How the riotous flock were ever got into their beds no one knows. The lads caroused until long past midnight, and no knocking on the walls of paternal boots, or whispered entreaties of maternal voices through keyholes, had any effect, for it was impossible to resist the present advantages for a grand Christmas rampage.

The girls giggled and gossiped, told secrets, and laid plans more quietly; while the small things tumbled into bed, and went to sleep at once, quite used up with the festivities of this remarkable day.

Grandma, down in her own cozy room, sat listening to the blithe noises with a smile on her face, for the past seemed to have come back again, and her own boys and girls to be frolicking above there, as they used to do forty years ago.

"It's all so beautiful I can't go to bed, Dolly, and lose any of it. They'll go away tomorrow, and I may never see them any more," she said, as Dolly tied on her nightcap and brought her slippers.

"Yes, you will, mum. That dear child has made it so pleasant they can't keep away. You'll see plenty of 'em, if they carry out half the plans they have made. Mrs. George wants to come up and pass the summer here; Mr. Tom says he shall send his boys to school here, and every girl among them has promised Kate to make her a long visit. The thing is done, mum, and you'll never be lonely any more."

"Thank God for that!" and Grandma bent her head as if she had received a great blessing. "Dolly, I want to go and look at those children. It seems so like a dream to have them here, I must be sure of it," said Grandma, folding her wrapper about her, and getting up with great decision.

"Massy on us, mum, you haven't been up them stairs for months. The dears are all right, warm as toasts, and sleepin' like dormice, I'll warrant," answered Dolly, taken aback at this new whim of old madam's.

But Grandma would go, so Dolly gave her an arm, and together the two old friends hobbled up the wide stairs, and peeped in at the precious children. The lads looked like a camp of weary warriors reposing after a victory, and Grandma went laughing away when she had taken a proud survey of this promising portion of the rising generation. The nursery was like a little convent full of rosy nuns sleeping peacefully; while a pictured Saint Agnes, with her lamb, smiled on them from the wall, and the firelight flickered over the white figures and sweet faces, as if the sight were too fair to be lost in darkness. The little ones lay about promiscuously, looking like dissipated Cupids with sugar hearts and faded roses still clutched in their chubby hands.

"My darlings!" whispered Grandma, lingering fondly over them to cover a pair of rosy feet, put back a pile of tumbled curls, or kiss a little mouth still smiling in its sleep.

But when she came to the coldest corner of the room, where Kate lay on the hardest mattress, under the thinnest quilt, the old lady's eyes were full of tender tears; and, forgetting the stiff joints that bent so painfully, she knelt slowly down, and, putting her arms about the girl, blessed her in silence for the happiness she had given one old heart.

Kate woke at once, and started up, exclaiming with a smile:

"Why, Grandma, I was dreaming about an angel, and you look like one with your white gown and silvery hair!"

"No, dear, you are the angel in this house. How can I ever give you up?" answered madam, holding fast the treasure that came to her so late.

"You never need to, Grandma, for I have made my choice."

TESSA'S SURPRISES

from *Aunt Jo's Scrap Bag*
(Volume I), 1871

In those days in Boston, where the gap between the comfortably rich and the very poor was large and wide, Louisa learned to make acquaintance with many young persons who were struggling with the desperate problems of extreme poverty. It was possible, as one went about, to catch glimpses of a girl singing and a boy making music in the hope of some return from friendly passers-by. We can imagine Louisa catching sight of such a pair and going on her way, making, in her immediate fancy, this story of what she hoped might come to them.

TESSA'S SURPRISES

I

Little Tessa sat alone by the fire, waiting for her father to come home from work. The children were fast asleep, all four in the big bed behind the curtain; the wind blew hard outside, and the snow beat on the windowpanes; the room was large and the fire so small and feeble that it didn't half warm the little bare toes peeping out of the old shoes on the hearth.

Tessa's father was an Italian plaster-worker, very poor, but kind and honest. The mother had died not long ago, and left twelve-year-old Tessa to take care of the little children. She tried to be very wise and motherly, and worked for them like any little woman; but it was so hard to keep the small bodies warm and fed, and the small souls good and happy, that poor Tessa was often at her wits' end. She always waited for her father, no matter how tired she was, so that he might find his supper warm, a bit of fire, and a loving little face to welcome him. Tessa thought over her troubles at these quiet times, and made her plans; for her father left things to her a good deal, and she had no friends but Tommo, the harp-boy upstairs, and the lively cricket who lived in the chimney. Tonight her face was very sober, and her pretty brown eyes very thoughtful as she stared at the fire and knit her brows, as if perplexed. She was not thinking of her old shoes, nor the empty closet, nor the boys' ragged clothes just then. No; she had a fine plan in her good little head, and was trying to discover how she could carry it out.

You see, Christmas was coming in a week; and she had set her heart on putting something in the children's stockings, as the mother used to do, for while she lived things were comfortable. Now Tessa had not a penny in the world, and didn't know how to get one, for all the father's earnings had to go for food, fire, and rent.

"If there were only fairies, ah! How heavenly that would be; for then I should tell them all I wish, and, pop! Behold the fine things in my lap!" said Tessa to herself. "I must earn the money; there is no one to give it to me, and I cannot beg. But what can I do, so small and stupid and shy as I am? I *must* find some way to give the little ones a nice Christmas. I *must!* I *must!*" and Tessa pulled her long hair, as if that would help her think.

But it didn't, and her heart got heavier and heavier; for it did seem hard that in a great city full of fine things, there should be none for poor Nono, Sep, and little Speranza. Just as Tessa's tears began to tumble off her eyelashes on to her brown cheeks, the cricket began to chirp. Of course, he didn't say a word; but it really did seem as if he had answered her question almost as well as a fairy; for, before he had piped a dozen shrill notes, an idea popped into Tessa's head — such a truly splendid idea that she clapped her hands and burst out laughing. "I'll do it! I'll do it! If father will let me," she said to herself, smiling and nodding at the fire. "Tommo will like to have me go with him and sing, while he plays his harp in the streets. I know many songs, and may get money if I am not frightened; for people throw pennies to other little girls who only play the tambourine. Yes, I will try; and then, if I do well, the little ones shall have a Merry Christmas."

So full of her plan was Tessa that she ran upstairs at once, and asked Tommo if he would take her with him on the morrow. Her friend was delighted, for he thought Tessa's songs very sweet, and was sure she would get money if she tried.

"But see, then, it is cold in the streets; the wind bites, and the snow freezes one's fingers. The day is very long, people are cross, and at night one is ready to die with weariness. Thou art so small, Tessa, I am afraid it will go badly with thee," said Tommo, who was a merry, black-eyed boy of fourteen, with the kindest heart in the world under his old jacket.

"I do not mind cold and wet, and cross people, if I can get the pennies," answered Tessa, feeling very brave with such a friend to help her. She thanked Tommo, and ran away to get ready, for she felt sure her father would not refuse her anything. She sewed up the holes in her shoes as well as she could, for she had much of that sort of cobbling to do; she mended her only gown, and laid ready the old hood and shawl which had been her mother's. Then she washed out little Ranza's frock and put it to dry, because she would not be able to do it the next day. She set the table and got things ready for breakfast, for Tommo went out early, and must not be kept waiting for her. She longed to make the beds and dress the children overnight, she was in such a hurry to have all in order; but, as that could not be, she sat down again, and tried over all the songs she knew. Six pretty ones were chosen; and she sang away with all her heart in a fresh little voice so sweetly that the children smiled in their sleep, and her father's tired face brightened as he entered, for Tessa was his cheery cricket on the hearth. When she had told her plan, Peter Benari shook his head, and thought it would never do; but Tessa begged so hard, he consented at last that she should try it for one week, and sent her to bed the happiest little girl in New York.

Next morning the sun shone, but the cold wind blew, and the snow lay thick in the streets. As soon as her father was gone, Tessa flew about and put everything in nice order, telling the children she was going out for the day, and they were to mind Tommo's mother, who would see about the fire and the dinner; for the good woman loved Tessa, and entered into her little plans with all her heart. Nono and Guiseppe, or Sep, as they called him, wondered what she was going away for, and little Ranza cried at being left; but Tessa told them they would know all about it in a week, and have a fine time if they were good; so they kissed her all round and let her go.

Poor Tessa's heart beat fast as she trudged away with Tommo, who slung his harp over his shoulder, and gave her his hand. It was rather a dirty hand, but so kind that Tessa clung to it, and kept looking up at the friendly brown face for encouragement.

"We go first to the *café*, where many French and Italians eat the breakfast. They like my music, and often give me sips of hot coffee, which I like much. You too shall have the sips, and perhaps the pennies, for these people are greatly kind," said Tommo, leading her into a large smoky place, where many people sat at little tables, eating and drinking. "See, now, have no fear; give them 'Bella Monica'; that is merry and will make the laugh," whispered Tommo, tuning his harp.

For a moment Tessa felt so frightened that she wanted to run away; but she remembered the empty stockings at home, and the fine plan, and she resolved *not* to give it up. One fat old Frenchman nodded to her, and it seemed to help her very much; for she began to sing before she thought, and that was the hardest part of it. Her voice trembled, and her cheeks grew redder and redder as she went on; but she kept her eyes fixed on her old shoes, and so got through without breaking down, which was very nice. The people laughed, for the song *was* merry; and the fat man smiled and nodded again. This gave her courage to try another, and she sang better and better each time; for Tommo played his best, and kept whispering to her, "Yes; we go well; this is fine. They will give the money and the blessed coffee."

So they did; for, when the little concert was over, several men put pennies in the cap Tessa offered, and the fat man took her on his knee, and ordered a mug of coffee, and some bread and butter for them both. This quite won her heart; and when they left the *café*, she kissed her hand to the old Frenchman, and said to her friend, "How kind they are! I like this very much; and now it is not hard."

But Tommo shook his curly head, and answered, soberly, "Yes, I took you there first, for they love music, and are of our country; but up among the great houses we shall not always do well. The people there are busy or hard or idle, and care nothing for harps and songs. Do not skip and laugh too soon, for the day is long, and we have but twelve pennies yet."

Tessa walked more quietly, and rubbed her cold hands, feeling that the world was a very big place, and wondering how the children got on at home without the little mother. Till noon they did not earn much, for everyone seemed in a hurry, and the noise of many sleigh-bells drowned the music. Slowly they made their way up to the great squares where the big houses were, with fine ladies and pretty children at the windows. Here Tessa sang all her best songs, and Tommo played as fast as his fingers could fly; but it was too cold to have the windows open, so the pretty children could not listen long, and the ladies tossed out a little money, and soon went back to their own affairs.

All the afternoon the two friends wandered about, singing and playing, and gathering up their small harvest. At dusk they went home — Tessa so hoarse she could hardly speak, and so tired she fell asleep over her supper. But she had made half a dollar, for Tommo divided the money fairly, and she felt rich with her share. The other days were very much like this; sometimes they made more, sometimes less, but Tommo always "went halves"; and Tessa kept on, in spite of cold and weariness, for her plans grew as her earnings increased, and now she hoped to get useful things, instead of candy and toys alone.

On the day before Christmas she made herself as tidy as she could, for she hoped to earn a good deal. She tied a bright scarlet handkerchief over the old hood, and the brilliant color set off her brown cheeks and bright eyes, as well as the pretty black braids of her hair. Tommo's mother lent her a pair of boots so big that they turned up at the toes, but there were no holes in them, and Tessa felt quite elegant in whole boots. Her hands were covered with chilblains, for she had no mittens; but she put them under her shawl, and scuffled merrily away in her big boots, feeling so glad that the week was over, and nearly three dollars safe in her pocket. How gay the streets were that day! How brisk everyone was, and how bright the faces looked, as people trotted about with big baskets, holly wreaths, and young evergreens going to blossom into splendid Christmas trees!

"If I could have a tree for the children, I'd never want anything again. But I can't; so I'll fill the socks all full, and be happy," said Tessa, as she looked wistfully into the gay stores, and saw the heavy baskets go by.

"Who knows what may happen if we do well?" returned Tommo, nodding wisely, for he had a plan as well as Tessa, and kept chuckling over it as he trudged through the mud. They did *not* do well, somehow, for people seemed so full of their own affairs they could not stop to listen, even to "Bella Monica," but bustled away to spend their money on turkeys, toys, and trees. In the afternoon it began to rain, and poor Tessa's heart to fail her; for the big boots tired her feet, the cold wind made her hands ache, and the rain spoiled the fine red handkerchief. Even Tommo looked sober, and didn't whistle as he walked, for he also was disappointed, and his plan looked rather doubtful, the pennies came in so slowly.

"We'll try one more street, and then go home, thou art so tired, little one. Come; let me wipe thy face, and give me thy hand here in my jacket pocket; there it will be as warm as any kitten"; and kind Tommo brushed away the drops which were not *all* rain from Tessa's cheeks, tucked the poor hand into his ragged pocket, and led her carefully along the slippery streets, for the boots nearly tripped her up.

II

At the first house, a cross old gentleman flapped his newspaper at them; at the second, a young gentleman and lady were so busy talking that they never turned their heads; and at the third, a servant came out and told them to go away, because someone was sick. At the fourth, some people let them sing all their songs, and gave nothing. The next three houses were empty; and the last of all showed not a single face, as they looked up anxiously. It was so cold, so dark and discouraging, that Tessa couldn't help one sob; and, as he glanced down at the little red nose and wet figure beside him, Tommo gave his harp an angry thump, and said something very fierce in Italian. They were just going to turn away; but they didn't, for that angry thump happened to be the best thing they could have done. All of a sudden a little head appeared at the window, as if the sound had brought it; then another and another, till there were five, of all heights and colors, and five eager faces peeped out, smiling and nodding to the two below.

"Sing, Tessa; sing! Quick! Quick!" cried Tommo, twanging away with all his might, and showing his white teeth, as he smiled back at the little gentlefolk.

Bless us! How Tessa did tune up at that! She chirped away like a real bird, forgetting all about the tears on her cheeks, the ache in her hands, and the heaviness at her heart. The children laughed, and clapped their hands, and cried "More! More! Sing another, little girl! Please, do!" And away they went again, piping and playing, till Tessa's breath was gone, and Tommo's stout fingers tingled well.

"Mamma says, come to the door; it's too muddy to throw the money in the street!" cried out a kindly child's voice, as Tessa held up the old cap, with beseeching eyes.

Up the wide stone steps went the street musicians, and the whole flock came running down to give a handful of silver, and ask all sorts of questions. Tessa felt so grateful, that, without waiting for Tommo, she sang her sweetest little song all alone. It was about a lost lamb, and her heart was in the song; therefore, she sang it well, so well, that a pretty young lady came down to listen, and stood watching the bright-eyed child, who looked about her as she sang, evidently enjoying the light and warmth of the fine hall, and the sight of the lovely children with their gay dresses, shining hair, and dainty little shoes.

"You have a charming voice, child. Who taught you to sing?" asked the young lady, kindly.

"My mother. She is dead now; but I do not forget," answered Tessa, in her pretty broken English.

"I wish she could sing at our tree, since Bella is ill," cried one of the children, peeping through the banisters.

"She is not fair enough for the angel, and too large to go up in the tree. But she sings sweetly, and looks as if she would like to see a tree," said the young lady.

"Oh, so much!" exclaimed Tessa; adding eagerly, "my sister Ranza is small and pretty as a baby-angel. She could sit up in the fine tree, and I could sing for her from under the table."

"Sit down and warm yourself, and tell me about Ranza," said the kind elder sister, who liked the confiding little girl, in spite of her shabby clothes.

So Tessa sat down and dried the big boots over the furnace, and told her story, while Tommo stood modestly in the background, and the children listened with faces full of interest.

"Oh, Rose! Let us see the little girl; and if she will do, let us have her, and Tessa can learn our song, and it will be splendid!" cried the biggest boy, who sat astride of a chair, and stared at the harp with round eyes.

"I'll ask Mamma," said Rose; and away she went into the dining room close by. As the door opened, Tessa saw what looked to her like a fairy feast — all silver mugs and flowery plates and oranges and nuts and rosy wine in tall glass pitchers, and smoking dishes

that smelt so deliciously she could not restrain a little sniff of satisfaction.

"Are you hungry?" asked the boy, in a grand tone.

"Yes, sir," meekly answered Tessa.

"I say, Mamma; she wants something to eat. Can I give her an
orange?" called the boy, prancing away into the splendid room,
quite like a fairy prince, Tessa thought.

A plump, motherly lady came out and looked at Tessa, asked a
few questions, and then told her to come tomorrow with Ranza,
and they would see what could be done. Tessa clapped her hands
for joy — she didn't mind the chilblains now — and Tommo
played a lively march, he was so pleased.

"Will you come, too, and bring your harp? You shall be paid,
and shall have something from the tree, likewise," said the motherly lady, who liked what Tessa gratefully told about his kindness
to her.

"Ah, yes; I shall come with much gladness, and play as never in
my life before," cried Tommo, with a flourish of the old cap that
made the children laugh.

"Give these to your brothers," said the fairy prince, stuffing
nuts and oranges into Tessa's hands.

"And these to the little girl," added one of the young princesses,
flying out of the dining room with cakes and rosy apples for
Ranza.

Tessa didn't know what to say; but her eyes were full, and she
just took the mother's white hand in both her little grimy ones,
and kissed it many times in her pretty Italian fashion. The lady
understood her, and stroked her cheek softly, saying to her elder
daughter, "We must take care of this good little creature. Freddy,
bring me your mittens; these poor hands must be covered. Alice,
get your play-hood; this handkerchief is all wet; and, Maud, bring
the old chinchilla tippet."

The children ran, and in a minute there were lovely blue mittens

on the red hands, a warm hood over the black braids, and a soft
"pussy" round the sore throat.

"Ah! so kind, so very kind! I have no way to say 'thank you';
but Ranza shall be for you a heavenly angel, and I will sing my
heart out for your tree!" cried Tessa, folding the mittens as if she
would say a prayer of thankfulness if she knew how.

Then they went away, and the pretty children called after them,
"Come again, Tessa! Come again, Tommo!" Now the rain didn't
seem dismal, the wind cold, nor the way long, as they bought their
gifts and hurried home, for kind words and the sweet magic of
charity had changed all the world to them.

I think the good spirits who fly about on Christmas Eve, to help
the loving fillers of little stockings, smiled very kindly on Tessa as
she brooded joyfully over the small store of presents that seemed
so magnificent to her. All the goodies were divided evenly into
three parts and stowed away in father's three big socks, which
hung against the curtain. With her three dollars, she had got a
pair of shoes for Nono, a knit cap for Sep, and a pair of white
stockings for Ranza; to her she also gave the new hood; to Nono
the mittens; and to Sep the tippet.

"Now the dear boys can go out, and my Ranza will be ready for
the lady to see, in her nice new things," said Tessa, quite sighing
with pleasure to see how well the gifts looked pinned up beside the
bulging socks, which wouldn't hold them all. The little mother
kept nothing for herself but the pleasure of giving everything
away; yet I think she was both richer and happier than if she had
kept them all. Her father laughed as he had not done since the
mother died, when he saw how comically the old curtain had
broken out into boots and hoods, stockings and tippets.

"I wish I had a gold gown and a silver hat for thee, my Tessa,
thou art so good. May the saints bless and keep thee always!" said
Peter Benari tenderly, as he held his little daughter close, and gave
her the good-night kiss.

Tessa felt very rich as she crept under the faded counterpane, feeling as if she had received a lovely gift, and fell happily asleep with chubby Ranza in her arms, and the two rough black heads peeping out at the foot of the bed. She dreamed wonderful dreams that night, and woke in the morning to find real wonders before her eyes. She got up early, to see if the socks were all right, and there she found the most astonishing sight. Four socks, instead of three; and by the fourth, pinned out quite elegantly, was a little dress, evidently meant for her — a warm, woollen dress, all made, and actually with bright buttons on it. It nearly took her breath away; so did the new boots on the floor, and the funny long stocking like a gray sausage, with a wooden doll staring out at the top, as if she said, politely, "A Merry Christmas, ma'am!" Tessa screamed and danced in her delight, and up tumbled all the children to scream and dance with her, making a regular carnival on a small scale. Everybody hugged and kissed everybody else, offered sucks of orange, bites of cake, and exchanges of candy; everyone tried on the new things, and pranced about in them like a flock of peacocks. Ranza skipped to and fro airily, dressed in her white socks and the red hood; the boys promenaded in their little shirts, one with his creaking new shoes and mittens, the other in his gay cap and fine tippet; and Tessa put her dress straight on, feeling that her father's "gold gown" was not all a joke. In her long stocking she found all sorts of treasures; for Tommo had stuffed it full of queer things, and his mother had made gingerbread into every imaginable shape, from fat pigs to full omnibuses.

Dear me! What happy little souls they were that morning; and when they were quiet again, how like a fairy tale did Tessa's story sound to them. Ranza was quite ready to be an angel; and the boys promised to be marvelously good, if they were only allowed to see the tree at the "palace," as they called the great house.

Little Ranza was accepted with delight by the kind lady and her children, and Tessa learned the song quite easily. The boys *were* asked; and, after a happy day, the young Italians all returned, to play their parts at the fine Christmas party. Mamma and Miss

Rose drilled them all; and, when the folding doors flew open, one rapturous "Oh!" arose from the crowd of children gathered to the festival. I assure you, it was splendid; the great tree glittering with lights and gifts; and on her invisible perch up among the green boughs sat the little golden-haired angel, all in white, with downy wings, a shining crown on her head, and the most serene satisfaction in her blue eyes, as she stretched her chubby arms to those below, and smiled her baby smile at them. Before anyone could speak, a voice, as fresh and sweet as a lark's, sang the Christmas Carol so blithely that everyone stood still to hear, and then clapped till the little angel shook on her perch, and cried out, "Be 'till, or me'll fall!" How they laughed at that; and what fun they had talking to Ranza, while Miss Rose stripped the tree, for the angel could not resist temptation, and amused herself by eating all the bonbons she could reach, till she was taken down, to dance about like a fairy in a white frock and red shoes. Tessa and her friends had many presents; the boys were perfect lambs, Tommo played for the little folks to dance, and everyone said something friendly to the strangers, so that they did not feel shy, in spite of shabby clothes. It was a happy night; and all their lives they remembered it as something too beautiful and bright to be quite true. Before they went home, the kind mamma told Tessa she should be her friend, and gave her a motherly kiss, which warmed the child's heart and seemed to set a seal upon that promise. It was faithfully kept, for the rich lady had been touched by Tessa's patient struggles and sacrifices; and for many years, thanks to her benevolence, there was no end to Tessa's Surprises.

MOUNTAIN LAUREL
AND MAIDENHAIR

from *A Garland for Girls*, 1886

Walpole, New Hampshire was a place of bold scenery and wide views, with rocky hillsides covered with rough grass, sweet fern and, in its own season, the glorious pink of mountain laurel. The Alcotts had relatives who lived there. Louisa's whole family spent a winter there, and it was from Walpole that Louisa set out for the first time to go to Boston to look for work, any work which she could do to earn enough to take care of herself and make her family more comfortable. She made many visits there through the years, and speaks in her journal of Walpole as being the inspiration of other stories, as it very plainly was of this one which she was writing at the beginning of 1886.

MOUNTAIN LAUREL
AND MAIDENHAIR

"Here's your breakfast, miss. I hope it's right. Your mother showed me how to fix it, and said I'd find a cup up here."

"Take that blue one. I have not much appetite, and can't eat if things are not nice and pretty. I like the flowers. I've been longing for some ever since I saw them last night."

The first speaker was a red-haired, freckle-faced girl, in a brown calico dress and white apron, with a tray in her hands and an air of timid hospitality in her manner; the second a pale, pretty creature, in a white wrapper and blue net, sitting in a large chair, looking about her with the languid interest of an invalid in a new place. Her eyes brightened as they fell upon a glass of rosy laurel and delicate maidenhair fern that stood among the toast and eggs, strawberries and cream, on the tray.

"Our laurel is jest in blow, and I'm real glad you come in time to see it. I'll bring you a lot, as soon's ever I get time to go for it."

As she spoke, the plain girl replaced the ugly crockery cup and saucer with the pretty china ones pointed out to her, arranged the dishes, and waited to see if anything else was needed.

"What is your name, please?" asked the pretty girl, refreshing herself with a draught of new milk.

"Rebecca. Mother thought I'd better wait on you; the little girls are so noisy and apt to forget. Wouldn't you like a piller to your back? You look so kind of feeble seems as if you wanted to be propped up a mite."

There was so much compassion and goodwill in the face and voice that Emily accepted the offer, and let Rebecca arrange a cushion behind her; then, while the one ate daintily, and the other stirred about an inner room, the talk went on — for two girls are seldom long silent when together.

"I think the air is going to suit me, for I slept all night and never woke till Mamma had been up ever so long and got things all nicely settled," said Emily, graciously, when the fresh straw-berries had been enjoyed, and the bread and butter began to vanish.

"I'm real glad you like it; most folks do, if they don't mind it being plain and quiet up here. It's gayer down at the hotel, but the air ain't half so good, and delicate folks generally like our old place best," answered Becky, as she tossed over a mattress and shook out the sheets with a brisk, capable air pleasant to see.

"I wanted to go to the hotel, but the doctor said it would be too noisy for me, so Mamma was glad to find rooms here. I didn't think a farmhouse *could* be so pleasant. That view is perfectly splendid!" and Emily sat up to gaze delightedly out of the win-dow, below which spread the wide intervale, through which the river ran with hay fields on either side, while along the green slopes of the hills lay farmhouses with garden plots, and big barns waiting for the harvest; and beyond, the rocky, wooded pastures dotted with cattle and musical with cowbells, brooks, and birds.

A balmy wind kissed a little color into the pale cheeks, the list-less eyes brightened as they looked, and the fretful lines vanished from lips that smiled involuntarily at the sweet welcome Nature gave the city child come to rest and play and grow gay and rosy in her green lap.

Becky watched her with interest, and was glad to see how soon the newcomer felt the charm of the place, for the girl loved her mountain home, and thought the old farmhouse the loveliest spot in the world.

"When you get stronger I can show you lots of nice views

around here. There's a woodsy place behind the house that's just lovely. Down by the laurel bushes is *my* favorite spot, and among the rocks is a cave where I keep things handy when I get a resting-spell now and then, and want to be quiet. Can't get much at home, when there's boarders and five children around in vacation time."

Becky laughed as she spoke, and there was a sweet motherly look in her plain face, as she glanced at the three little red heads bobbing about the dooryard below, where hens cackled, a pet lamb fed, and the old white dog lay blinking in the sun.

"I like children; we have none at home, and Mamma makes such a baby of me I'm almost ashamed sometimes. I want her to have a good rest now, for she has taken care of me all winter and needs it. You shall be my nurse, if I need one; but I hope to be so well soon that I can see to myself. It's so tiresome to be ill!" and Emily sighed as she leaned back among her pillows, with a glance at the little glass which showed her a thin face and shorn head.

"It must be! I never was sick, but I have taken care of sick folks, and have a sight of sympathy for 'em. Mother says I make a pretty good nurse, being strong and quiet," answered Becky, plumping up pillows and folding towels with a gentle dispatch which was very grateful to the invalid, who had dreaded a noisy, awkward serving-maid.

"Never ill! How nice that must be! I'm always having colds and headaches, and fusses of some kind. What do you do to keep well, Rebecca?" asked Emily, watching her with interest, as she came in to remove the tray.

"Nothing but work; I haven't time to be sick, and when I'm tuckered out, I go and rest over yonder. Then I'm all right, and buckle to again, as smart as ever," and every freckle in Becky's rosy face seemed to shine with cheerful strength and courage.

"I'm 'tuckered out' doing nothing," said Emily, amused with the new expression, and eager to try a remedy which showed such fine results in this case. "I shall visit your pet places and do a little work as soon as I am able, and see if it won't set me up. Now I can only dawdle, doze, and read a little. Will you please put those books here on the table? I shall want them by and by."

Emily pointed to a pile of blue and gold volumes lying on a trunk, and Becky dusted her hands as she took them up with an air of reverence, for she read on the backs of the volumes names which made her eyes sparkle.

"Do you care for poetry?" asked Emily, surprised at the girl's look and manner.

"Guess I do! don't get much except the pieces I cut out of papers, but I love 'em, and stick 'em in an old ledger, and keep it down in my cubby among the rocks. I do love *that* man's pieces. They seem to go right to the spot somehow." And Becky smiled at the name of Whittier as if the sweetest of our poets was a dear old friend of hers.

"I like Tennyson better. Do you know him?" asked Emily, with a superior air, for the idea of this farmer's daughter knowing anything about poetry amused her.

"Oh yes, I've got a number of his pieces in my book, and I'm fond of 'em. But this man makes things so kind of true and natural I feel at home with *him*. And this one I've longed to read, though I guess I can't understand much of it. His 'Bumble Bee' was just lovely; with the grass and columbines and the yellow breeches of the bee. I'm never tired of that"; and Becky's face woke up into something like beauty as she glanced hungrily at the Emerson while she dusted the delicate cover that hid the treasures she coveted.

"I don't care much for him, but Mamma does. I like romantic poems, and ballads, and songs; don't like descriptions of clouds and fields, and bees, and farmers," said Emily, showing plainly that even Emerson's simplest poems were far above her comprehension as yet, because she loved sentiment more than Nature.

"I do, because I know 'em better than love and the romantic stuff most poetry tells about. But I don't pretend to judge, I'm glad of anything I can get. Now if you don't want me I'll pick up my dishes and go to work."

With that Becky went away, leaving Emily to rest and dream with her eyes on the landscape which was giving her better poetry than any her books held. She told her mother about the odd girl, and was sure she would be amusing if she did not forget her place and try to be friends.

"She is a good creature, my dear, her mother's mainstay, and works beyond her strength, I am sure. Be kind to the poor girl, and put a little pleasure into her life if you can," answered Mrs. Spenser, as she moved about, settling comforts and luxuries for her invalid.

"I shall *have* to talk to her, as there is no other person of my age in the house. How are the schoolmarms? Shall you get on with them, Mamma? It will be so lonely here for us both, if we don't make friends with someone."

"Most intelligent and amiable women all three, and we shall have pleasant times together, I am sure. You may safely cultivate Becky; Mrs. Taylor told me she was a remarkably bright girl, though she may not look it."

"Well, I'll see. But I do hate freckles and big red hands, and round shoulders. She can't help it, I suppose, but ugly things fret me."

"Remember that she has no time to be pretty, and be glad she is so neat and willing. Shall we read, dear? I'm ready now."

Emily consented, and listened for an hour or two while the pleasant voice beside her conjured away all her vapors with some of Mrs. Ewing's charming tales.

"The grass is dry now, and I want to stroll on that green lawn before lunch. You rest, Mamma dear, and let me make discoveries all alone," proposed Emily, when the sun shone warmly, and the instinct of all young creatures for air and motion called her out.

So, with her hat and wrap, and book and parasol, she set forth to explore the new land in which she found herself.

Down the wide, creaking stairs and out upon the door-stone she went, pausing there for a moment to decide where first to go. The sound of someone singing in the rear of the house led her in that direction, and turning the corner she made her first pleasant discovery. A hill rose steeply behind the farmhouse, and leaning from the bank was an old apple tree, shading a spring that trickled out from the rocks and dropped into a mossy trough below. Up the tree had grown a wild grapevine, making a green canopy over the great log which served as a seat, and someone had planted maidenhair ferns about both seat and spring to flourish beautifully in the damp, shady spot.

"Oh, how pretty! I'll go and sit there. It looks clean, and I can see what is going on in that big kitchen, and hear the singing. I suppose it's Becky's little sisters by the racket."

Emily established herself on the lichen-covered log with her feet upon a stone, and sat enjoying the musical tinkle of the water, with her eyes on the delicate ferns stirring in the wind, and the lively jingle of the multiplication table chanted by childish voices in her ear.

Presently two little girls with a great pan of beans came to do their work on the back doorstep, a third was seen washing dishes at a window, and Becky's brown-spotted gown flew about the kitchen as if a very energetic girl wore it. A woman's voice was heard giving directions, as the speaker was evidently picking chickens somewhere out of sight.

A little of the talk reached Emily and both amused and annoyed her, for it proved that the country people were not as stupid as they looked.

"Oh, well, we mustn't mind if she *is* notional and kind of wearing; she's been sick, and it will take time to get rid of her fretty ways. Jest be pleasant, and take no notice, and that nice mother of hers will make it all right," said the woman's voice.

"How anybody with every mortal thing to be happy with *can* be out-of-sorts passes me. She fussed about every piller, chair, trunk, and mite of food last night, and kept that poor tired lady trotting till I was provoked. She's right pleasant this morning though, and as pretty as a picture in her ruffled gown and that blue thing on her head," answered Becky from the pantry, as she rattled out the pie-board, little dreaming who sat hidden behind the grapevine festoons that veiled the corner by the spring.

"Well, she's got redder hair'n' we have, so she needn't be so grand and try to hide it with blue nets," added one little voice.

"Yes, and it's ever so much shorter 'n' ours, and curls all over her head like Daisy's wool. I should think such a big girl would feel real ashamed without no braids," said the other child, proudly surveying the tawny mane that hung over her shoulders — for like most red-haired people all the children were blessed with luxuriant crops of every shade from golden auburn to regular carrots.

"I think it's lovely. Suppose it had to be cut off when she had the fever. Wish I could get rid of my mop, it's such a bother," and Becky was seen tying a clean towel over the great knot that made her head look very like a copper kettle.

"Now fly round, dearie, and get them pies ready. I'll have these fowls on in a minute, and then go to my butter. You run off and see if you can't find some wild strawberries for the poor girl, soon's ever you are through with them beans, children. We must kind of pamper her up for a spell till her appetite comes back," said the mother.

Here the chat ended, and soon the little girls were gone, leaving Becky alone rolling out piecrust before the pantry window. As she worked her lips moved, and Emily, still peeping through the leaves, wondered what she was saying, for a low murmur rose and fell, emphasized now and then with a thump of the rolling-pin.

"I mean to go and find out. If I stand on that wash-bench I can look in and see her work. I'll show them all that I'm *not* 'fussy,' and can be 'right pleasant' if I like."

With this wise resolution Emily went down the little path, and after pausing to examine the churn set out to dry, and the row of pans shining on a neighboring shelf, made her way to the window, mounted the bench while Becky's back was turned, and pushing away the morning-glory vines and scarlet beans that ran up on either side peeped in with such a smiling face that the crossest cook could not have frowned on her as an intruder.

"May I see you work? I can't eat pies, but I like to watch people make them. Do you mind?"

"Not a bit. I'd ask you to come in, but it's dreadful hot here, and not much room," answered Becky, crimping round the pastry before she poured in the custard. "I'm going to make a nice little pudding for you; your mother said you liked 'em; or would you rather have whipped cream with a mite of jelly in it?" asked Becky, anxious to suit her new boarder.

"Whichever is easiest to make. I don't care what I eat. Do tell me what you were saying. It sounded like poetry," said Emily, leaning both elbows on the wide ledge with a pale pink morning glory kissing her cheek, and a savory odor reaching her nose.

"Oh, I was mumbling some verses. I often do when I work, it sort of helps me along; but it must sound dreadfully silly," and Becky blushed as if caught in some serious fault.

"I do it, and it's a great comfort when I lie awake. I should think you *would* want something to help you along, you work so hard. Do you like it, Becky?"

The familiar name, the kind tone, made the plain face brighten with pleasure as its owner said, while she carefully filled a pretty bowl with a golden mixture rich with fresh eggs and country milk:

"No, I don't, but I ought to. Mother isn't as strong as she used to be, and there's a sight to do, and the children to be brought up, and the mortgage to be paid off; so if *I* don't fly round, who will? We are doing real well now, for Mr. Walker manages the farm and gives us our share, so our living is all right; then boarders in summer and my school in winter helps a deal, and every year the boys can do more, so I'd be a real sinner to complain if I do have to step lively all day."

Becky smiled as she spoke, and straightened her bent shoulders as if settling her burden for another trudge along the path of duty.

"Do you keep school? Why, how old are you, Becky?" asked Emily, much impressed by this new discovery.

"I'm eighteen. I took the place of a teacher who got sick last fall, and I kept school all winter. Folks seemed to like me, and I'm going to have the same place this year. I'm so glad, for I needn't go away, and the pay is pretty good, as the school is large and the children do well. You can see the schoolhouse down the valley, that red brick one where the roads meet." And Becky pointed a floury finger, with an air of pride that was pleasant to see.

Emily glanced at the little red house where the sun shone hotly in summer, and all the winds of heaven must rage wildly in wintertime, for it stood, as country schools usually do, in the barest, most uninviting spot for miles around.

"Isn't it awful down there in winter?" she asked, with a shiver at the idea of spending days shut up in that forlorn place, with a crowd of rough country children.

"Pretty cold, but we have plenty of wood, and we are used to snow and gales up here. We often coast down, the whole lot of us, and that is great fun. We take our dinners and have games noon-spells, and so we get on first-rate; some of my boys are big fellows, older than I am; they clear the roads and make the fire and look after us, and we are real happy together."

Emily found it so impossible to imagine happiness under such circumstances that she changed the subject by asking in a tone which had unconsciously grown more respectful since this last revelation of Becky's abilities:

"If you do so well here, why don't you try for a larger school in a better place?"

"Oh, I couldn't leave mother yet; I hope to some day, when the girls are older, and the boys able to get on alone. But I can't go now, for there's a sight of things to do, and mother is always laid up with rheumatism in cold weather. So much butter-making down cellar is bad for her; but she won't let me do that in summer, so I take care of her in winter. I can see to things night and morning, and through the day she's quiet, and sits piecing carpet-rags and resting up for next spring. We made and wove all the carpets in the house, except the parlor one. Mrs. Taylor gave us that, and the curtains, and the easy-chair. Mother takes a sight of comfort in that."

"Mrs. Taylor is the lady who first came to board here, and told us and others about it," said Emily.

"Yes, and she's the kindest lady in the world! I'll tell you all about her some day, it's real interesting; now I must see to my pies, and get the vegetables on," answered Becky, glancing at the gay clock in the kitchen with an anxious look.

"Then I won't waste any more of your precious time. May I sit in that pretty place; or is it your private bower?" asked Emily, as she dismounted from the wash-bench.

"Yes, indeed you may. That's mother's resting place when work is done. Father made the spring long ago, and I put the ferns there. She can't go rambling around, and she likes pretty things, so we fixed it up for her, and she takes comfort there nights."

Becky bustled off to the oven with her pies, and Emily roamed away to the big barn to lie on the hay, enjoying the view down the valley, as she thought over what she had seen and heard, and very naturally contrasted her own luxurious and tenderly guarded life with this other girl's, so hard and dull and narrow. Working all summer and teaching all winter in that dismal little schoolhouse, with no change but home cares and carpet weaving! It looked horrible to pleasure-loving Emily, who led the happy, carefree life of girls of her class, with pleasures of all sorts, and a future of still greater luxury, variety, and happiness opening brightly before her.

It worried her to think of anyone being contented with such a meagre share of the good things of life, when she was unsatisfied in spite of the rich store showered upon her. She could not understand it, and fell asleep wishing everyone could be comfortable — it was so annoying to see them grubbing in kitchens, teaching in bleak schoolhouses among snowdrifts, and wearing ugly calico gowns.

A week or two of quiet, country fare, and the bracing mountain air worked wonders for the invalid, and everyone rejoiced to see the pale cheeks begin to grow round and rosy, the languid eyes to brighten, and the feeble girl who used to lie on her sofa half the day now go walking about with her alpenstock, eager to explore all the pretty nooks among the hills. Her mother blessed Mrs. Taylor for suggesting this wholesome place. The tired "schoolmarms," as Emily called the three young women who were their fellow-boarders, congratulated her as well as themselves on the daily improvement in strength and spirits all felt; and Becky exulted in the marvelous effects of her native air, aided by mother's good cookery and the cheerful society of the children, whom the good girl considered the most remarkable and lovable youngsters in the world.

Emily felt like the queen of this little kingdom, and was regarded as such by everyone, for with returning health she lost her fretful ways, and living with simple people, soon forgot her girlish airs and vanities, becoming very sweet and friendly with all about her. The children considered her a sort of good fairy who could grant wishes with magical skill, as various gifts plainly proved. The boys were her devoted servants, ready to run errands, "hitch up" and take her to drive at any hour, or listen in mute delight when she sang to her guitar in the summer twilight.

But to Becky she was a special godsend and comfort, for before the first month had gone they were good friends, and Emily had made a discovery which filled her head with brilliant plans for Becky's future, in spite of her mother's warnings, and the sensible girl's own reluctance to be dazzled by enthusiastic prophecies and dreams.

It came about in this way. Some three weeks after the two girls met, Emily went one evening to their favorite trysting-place, — Becky's bower among the laurels. It was a pretty nook in the shadow of a great gray boulder near the head of the green valley which ran down to spread into the wide intervale below. A brook went babbling among the stones and grass and sweet ferns, while all the slope was rosy with laurel flowers in their times, as the sturdy bushes grew thickly on the hillside, down the valley, and among the woods that made a rich background for these pink and white bouquets arranged with Nature's own careless grace.

Emily liked this spot, and ever since she had been strong enough to reach it, loved to climb up and sit there with book and work, enjoying the lovely panorama before her. Floating mists often gave her a constant succession of pretty pictures; now a sunny glimpse of the distant lake, then the church spire peeping above the hill, or a flock of sheep feeding in the meadow, a gay procession of young pilgrims winding up the mountain, or a black cloud heavy with a coming storm, welcome because of the glorious rainbow and its shadow which would close the pageant.

Unconsciously the girl grew to feel not only the beauty but the value of these quiet hours, to find a new peace, refreshment, and happiness, bubbling up in her heart as naturally as the brook gushed out among the mossy rocks, and went singing away through hayfields and gardens, and by dusty roads, till it met the river and rolled on to the sea. Something dimly stirred in her, and the healing spirit that haunts such spots did its sweet ministering till the innocent soul began to see that life was not perfect without labor as well as love, duty as well as happiness, and that true contentment came from within, not from without.

On the evening we speak of, she went to wait for Becky, who would join her as soon as the after-supper chores were done. In the little cave which held a few books, a dipper, and a birch-bark basket for berries, Emily kept a sketching block and a box of pencils, and often amused herself by trying to catch some of the lovely scenes before her. These efforts usually ended in a humbler attempt, and a good study of an oak tree, a bit of rock, or a clump of ferns was the result. This evening the sunset was so beautiful she could not draw, and remembering that somewhere in Becky's scrapbook there was a fine description of such an hour by some poet, she pulled out the shabby old volume, and began to turn over the leaves.

She had never cared to look at it but once, having read all the best of its contents in more attractive volumes, so Becky kept it tucked away in the farther corner of her rustic closet, and evidently thought it a safe place to conceal a certain little secret which Emily now discovered. As she turned the stiff pages filled with all sorts of verses, good, bad, and indifferent, a sheet of paper appeared on which was scribbled these lines in schoolgirl handwriting:

MOUNTAIN LAUREL

My bonnie flower, with truest joy
Thy welcome face I see,
The world grows brighter to my eyes,
And summer comes with thee.
My solitude now finds a friend,
And after each hard day,
I in my mountain garden walk,
To rest, or sing, or pray.

All down the rocky slope is spread
Thy veil of rosy snow,
And in the valley by the brook,
Thy deeper blossoms grow.
The barren wilderness grows fair,
Such beauty dost thou give;

And human eyes and Nature's heart
    Rejoice that thou dost live.

Each year I wait thy coming, dear,
    Each year I love thee more,
For life grows hard, and much I need
    Thy honey for my store.
So, like a hungry bee, I sip
    Sweet lessons from thy cup,
And sitting at a flower's feet,
    My soul learns to look up.

No laurels shall I ever win,
    No splendid blossoms bear,
But gratefully receive and use
    God's blessed sun and air;
And, blooming where my lot is cast,
    Grow happy and content,
Making some barren spot more fair,
    For a humble life well spent.

"She wrote it herself! I can't believe it!" said Emily, as she put down the paper, looking rather startled, for she *did* believe it, and felt as if she had suddenly looked into a fellow-creature's heart. "I thought her just an ordinary girl, and here she is a poet, writing verses that make me want to cry! I don't suppose they *are* very good, but they seem to come right out of her heart, and touch me with the longing and the patience or the piety in them. Well, I *am* surprised!" and Emily read the lines again, seeing the faults more plainly than before, but still feeling that the girl put herself into them, vainly trying to express what the wild flower was to her in the loneliness which comes to those who have a little spark of the divine fire burning in their souls.

"Shall I tell her I've found it out? I must! and see if I can't get her verses printed. Of course she has more tucked away somewhere. That is what she hums to herself when she's at work, and won't tell me about when I ask. Sly thing! To be so bashful and hide her gift. I'll tease her a bit and see what she says. Oh dear, I wish *I* could do it! Perhaps she'll be famous some day, and then I'll have the glory of discovering her."

With that consolation Emily turned over the pages of the ledger and found several more bits of verse, some very good for an untaught girl, others very faulty, but all having a certain strength of feeling and simplicity of language unusual in the effusions of young maidens at the sentimental age.

Emily had a girlish admiration for talent of any kind, and being fond of poetry, was especially pleased to find that her humble friend possessed the power of writing it. Of course she exaggerated Becky's talent, and as she waited for her, felt sure that she had discovered a feminine Burns among the New Hampshire hills, for all the verses were about natural and homely objects, touched into beauty by sweet words or tender sentiment. She had time to build a splendid castle in the air and settle Becky in it with a crown of glory on her head, before the quiet figure in a faded sunbonnet came slowly up the slope with the glow of sunset on a tired but tranquil face.

"Sit here and have a good rest, while I talk to you," said Emily, eager to act the somewhat dramatic scene she had planned. Becky sank upon the red cushion prepared for her, and sat looking down at the animated speaker, as Emily, perched on a mossy stone before her, began the performance.

"Becky, did you ever hear of the Goodale children? They lived in the country and wrote poetry and grew to be famous."

"Oh yes, I've read their poems and like 'em very much. Do you know 'em?" and Becky looked interested at once.

"No, but I once met a girl who was something like them, only she didn't have such an easy time as they did, with a father to help, and a nice Sky-farm, and good luck generally. I've tried to write verses myself, but I always get into a muddle, and give it up. This makes me interested in other girls who *can* do it, and I want to help my friend. I'm *sure* she has talent, and I'd so like to give her a lift in some way. Let me read you a piece of hers and see what you think of it."

"Do!" and Becky threw off the sunbonnet, folded her hands round her knees, and composed herself to listen with such perfect unconsciousness of what was coming that Emily both laughed at the joke and blushed at the liberty she felt she was taking with the poor girl's carefully hidden secret.

Becky was sure now that Emily was going to read something of her own after this artful introduction, and began to smile as the paper was produced and the first four lines read in a tone that was half timid, half triumphant. Then with a cry she seized and crumpled up the paper, exclaiming almost fiercely:

"It's mine! Where did you get it? How dar'st you touch it?"

Emily fell upon her knees with a face and voice so full of penitence, pleasure, sympathy, and satisfaction, that Becky's wrath was appeased before her friend's explanation ended with these soothing and delightful words:

"That's all, dear, and I beg your pardon. But I'm sure you will be famous if you keep on, and I shall yet see a volume of poems by Rebecca Moore of Rocky Nook, New Hampshire."

Becky hid her face as if shame, surprise, wonder, and joy filled her heart too full and made a few happy tears drop on the hands so worn with hard work, when they ached to be holding a pen and trying to record the fancies that sang in her brain as ceaselessly as the soft sough of the pines or the ripple of the brook murmured in her ear when she sat here alone. She could not express the vague longings that stirred in her soul; she could only feel and dimly strive to understand and utter them, with no thought of fame or fortune — for she was a humble creature, and never knew that the hardships of her life were pressing out the virtues of her nature as the tread of careless feet crush the sweet perfume from wild herbs.

Presently she looked up, deeply touched by Emily's words and caresses, and her blue eyes shone like stars as her face beamed with something finer than mere beauty, for the secrets of her innocent heart were known to this friend now, and it was very sweet to accept the first draught of confidence and praise.

"I don't mind much, but I was scared for a minute. No one knows but Mother, and she laughs at me, though she don't care if it makes me happy. I'm glad you like my scribbling, but really I never think or hope of being anybody. I couldn't, you know! But it's real nice to have you say I *might* and to make believe for a while."

"But why not, Becky? The Goodale girls did, and half the poets in the world were poor, ignorant people at first, you know. It only needs time and help, and the gift will grow, and people see it; and then the glory and the money will come," cried Emily, quite carried away by her own enthusiasm and goodwill.

"Could I get any money by these things?" asked Becky, looking at the crumpled paper lying under a laurel bush.

"Of course you could, dear! Let me have some of them, and I'll show you that I know good poetry when I see it. You will believe if some bank-bills come with the paper the verses appear in, I hope?"

Blind to any harm she might do by exciting vain hopes in her eagerness to cheer and help, Emily made this rash proposal in all good faith, meaning to pay for the verses herself if no editor was found to accept them.

Becky looked half bewildered by this brilliant prospect, and took a long breath, as if some hand had lifted a heavy burden a little way from her weary back, for stronger than ambition for herself was love for her family, and the thought of help for them was sweeter than any dream of fame.

"Yes, I would! Oh, if I only *could*, I'd be the happiest girl in the world! But I can't believe it, Emily. I heard Mrs. Taylor say that only the *very best* poetry paid, and mine is poor stuff, I know well enough."

"Of course it needs polishing and practice and all that; but I'm sure it is oceans better than half the sentimental twaddle we see in the papers, and I *know* that some of those pieces *are* paid for, because I have a friend who is in a newspaper office, and he told me so. Yours are quaint and simple and some very original. I'm sure that ballad of the old house is lovely, and I want to send it to Whittier. Mamma knows him; it's the sort he likes, and he is so kind to everyone, he will criticize it, and be interested when she tells him about you. Do let me!"

"I never could in the world! It would be so bold, Mother would think I was crazy. I love Mr. Whittier, but I wouldn't dar'st to show him my nonsense, though reading his beautiful poetry helps me ever so much."

Becky looked and spoke as if her breath had been taken away by this audacious proposal; and yet a sudden delicious hope sprang up in her heart that there might, perhaps, be a spark of real virtue in the little fire which burned within her, warming and brightening her dull life.

"Let us ask Mamma; she will tell us what is best to do first, for she knows all sorts of literary people, and won't say any more than you want her to. I'm bent on having my way, Becky, and the more modest you are, the surer I am that you are a genius. Real geniuses always *are* shy; so you just make up your mind to give me the best of your pieces, and let me prove that I'm right."

It was impossible to resist such persuasive words, and Becky soon yielded to the little siren who was luring her out of her safe, small pool into the deeper water that looks so blue and smooth till the venturesome paper boats get into the swift eddies, or run aground upon the rocks and sandbars.

The greatest secrecy was to be preserved, and no one but Mrs. Spenser was to know what a momentous enterprise was afoot. The girls sat absorbed in their brilliant plans till it was nearly dark, then groped their way home hand in hand, leaving another secret for the laurels to keep and dream over through their long sleep, for blossom time was past, and the rosy faces turning pale in the July sun.

Neither of the girls forgot the talk they had that night in Emily's room, for she led her captive straight to her mother, and told her all their plans and aspirations without a moment's delay.

Mrs. Spenser much regretted her daughter's well-meant enthusiasm, but fearing harm might be done, very wisely tried to calm the innocent excitement of both by the quiet matter-of-fact way in which she listened to the explanation Emily gave her, read the verses timidly offered by Becky, and then said, kindly but firmly:

"This is not poetry, my dear girls, though the lines run smoothly enough, and the sentiment is sweet. It would bring neither fame nor money, and Rebecca puts more real truth, beauty, and poetry into her dutiful daily life than in any lines she has written."

"We had such a lovely plan for Becky to come to town with me, and see the world, and write, and be famous. How can you spoil it all?"

"My foolish little daughter, I must prevent you from spoiling this good girl's life by your rash projects. Becky will see that I am wise, though you do not, and *she* will understand this verse from my favorite poet, and lay it to heart:

> "So near is grandeur to our dust,
> So nigh is God to man,
> When Duty whispers low, 'Thou must!'
> The youth replies, 'I can!' "

"I do! I will! Please go on," and Becky's troubled eyes grew clear and steadfast as she took the words home to herself, resolving to live up to them.

"Oh, Mother!" cried Emily, thinking her very cruel to nip their budding hopes in this way.

"I know you won't believe it now, nor be able to see all that I mean perhaps, but time will teach you both to own that I am right, and to value the substance more than the shadow," continued Mrs. Spenser. "Many girls write verses and think they are poets; but it is only a passing mood, and fortunately for the world, and for them also, it soon dies out in some more genuine work or passion. Very few have the real gift, and those to whom it *is* given wait and work and slowly reach the height of their powers. Many delude themselves, and try to persuade the world that they can sing; but it is waste of time, and ends in disappointment, as the mass of sentimental rubbish we all see plainly proves. Write your little verses, my dear, when the spirit moves — it is a harmless pleasure, a real comfort, and a good lesson for you; but do not neglect higher duties or deceive yourself with false hopes and vain dreams. 'First live, then write,' is a good motto for ambitious young people. A still better for us all is, 'Do the duty that lies nearest,' and the faithful performance of that, no matter how humble it is, will be the best help for whatever talent may lie hidden in us, ready to bloom when the time comes. Remember this, and do not let my enthusiastic girl's well-meant but unwise prophecies and plans unsettle you, and unfit you for the noble work you are doing."

"Thank you, ma'am! I *will* remember; I know you are right, and I won't be upset by foolish notions. I never imagined before that I *could* be a poet; but it sounded so sort of splendid, I thought maybe it *might* happen to me, by and by, as it does to other folks. I won't lot on it, but settle right down and do my work cheerful."

As she listened, Becky's face had grown pale and serious, even a little sad; but as she answered, her eyes shone, her lips were firm, and her plain face almost beautiful with the courage and confidence that sprang up within her. She saw the wisdom of her friend's advice, felt the kindness of showing her the mistake frankly, and was grateful for it — conscious in her own strong, loving heart that it *was* better to live and work for others than to dream and strive for herself alone.

Mrs. Spenser was both surprised and touched by the girl's look, words, and manner, and her respect much increased by the courage and good temper with which she saw her lovely castle in the air vanish like smoke, leaving the hard reality looking harder than ever, after this little flight into the fairy regions of romance.

She talked long with the girls, and gave them the counsel all eager young people need, yet are very slow to accept till experience teaches them its worth. As the friend of many successful literary people, Mrs. Spenser was constantly receiving the confidences of unfledged scribblers, each of whom was sure that he or she had something valuable to add to the world's literature. Her advice was always the same, "Work and wait," and only now and then was a young poet or author found enough in earnest to do both, and thereby prove to themselves and others that either they *did* possess power, or did not, and so settle the question forever. "First live, then write," proved a *quietus* for many, and "Do the duty that lies nearest," satisfied the more sincere that they could be happy without fame. So, thanks to this wise and kindly woman, a large number of worthy youths and maidens ceased dreaming and fell to work, and the world was spared reams of feeble verse and third-rate romances.

After that night Becky spent fewer spare hours in her nest, and more in reading with Emily, who lent her books and helped her to understand them — both much assisted by Mrs. Spenser, who marked passages, suggested authors, and explained whatever puzzled them. Very happy bits of time were these, and very precious to both, as Emily learned to see and appreciate the humble, harder side of life, and Becky got delightful glimpses into the beautiful world of art, poetry, and truth, which gave her better food for heart and brain than sentimental musings or blind efforts to satisfy the hunger of her nature with verse-writing.

Their favorite places were in the big barn, on the front porch, or by the spring. This last was Emily's schoolroom, and she both taught and learned many useful lessons there.

One day as Becky came to rest a few minutes and shell peas, Emily put down her book to help; and as the pods flew, she said, nodding toward the delicate ferns that grew thickly all about the trough, the rock, and the grassy bank:

"We have these in our greenhouse, but I never saw them growing wild before, and I don't find them anywhere up here. How did you get such beauties, and make them do so well?"

"Oh, they grow in nooks on the mountain hidden under the taller ferns, and in sly corners. But they don't grow like these, and die soon unless transplanted and taken good care of. They always make me think of you — so graceful and delicate, and just fit to live with tea-roses in a hothouse, and go to balls in beautiful ladies' *bo*kays," answered Becky, smiling at her new friend, always so dainty, and still so delicate in spite of the summer's rustication.

"Thank you! I suppose I shall never be very strong or able to do much; so I *am* rather like a fern, and do live in a conservatory all winter, as I can't go out a great deal. An idle thing, Becky!" And Emily sighed, for she was born frail, and even her tenderly guarded life could not give her the vigor of other girls. But the sigh changed to a smile as she added:

"If I am like the fern, you are like your own laurel — strong, rosy, and able to grow anywhere. I want to carry a few roots home, and see if they won't grow in my garden. Then you will have me, and I you. I only hope *your* plant will do as well as mine does here."

"It won't! Ever so many folks have taken roots away, but they never thrive in gardens as they do on the hills where they belong. So I tell 'em to leave the dear bushes alone, and come up here and enjoy 'em in their own place. You might keep a plant of it in your hothouse, and it would blow I dare say; but it would never be half so lovely as my acres of them, and I guess it would only make you sad, seeing it so far from home, and pale and pining," answered Becky, with her eyes on the green slopes where the mountain laurel braved the wintry snow, and came out fresh and early in the spring.

"Then I'll let it alone till I come next summer. But don't you take any of the fern into the house in the cold weather? I should think it would grow in your sunny windows," said Emily, pleased by the fancy that it resembled herself.

"I tried it, but it needs a damp place, and our cold nights kill it. No, it won't grow in our old house; but I cover it with leaves, and the little green sprouts come up as hearty as can be out here. The shade, the spring, the shelter of the rock, keep it alive, you see, so it's no use trying to move it."

Both sat silent for a few minutes, as their hands moved briskly and they thought of their different lots. An inquisitive ray of sunshine peeped in at them, touching Becky's hair till it shone like red gold. The same ray dazzled Emily's eyes; she put up her hand to pull her hat-brim lower, and touched the little curls on her forehead. This recalled her pet grievance, and made her say impatiently, as she pushed the thick short locks under her net:

"My hair is *such* a plague! I don't know what I am to do when I go into society by and by. This crop is so unbecoming, and I can't match my hair anywhere, it is such a peculiar shade of golden-auburn."

"It's a pretty color, and I think the curls much nicer than a boughten switch," said Becky, quite unconscious that her own luxuriant locks were of the true Titian red, and would be much admired by artistic eyes.

"I don't! I shall send to Paris to match it, and then wear a braid round my head as you do sometimes. I suppose it will cost a fortune, but I *won't* have a strong-minded crop. A friend of mine got a lovely golden switch for fifty dollars."

"My patience! Do folks pay like that for false hair?" asked Becky, amazed.

"Yes, indeed. White hair costs a hundred, I believe, if it is long.

Why, you could get ever so much for yours if you ever wanted to sell it. I'll take part of it, for in a little while mine will be as dark, and I'd like to wear your hair, Becky."

"Don't believe Mother would let me. She is very proud of our red heads. If I ever do cut it, you shall have some. I may be hard up and glad to sell it perhaps. My sakes! I smell the cake burning!" And off flew Becky to forget the chat in her work.

Emily did not forget it, and hoped Becky would be tempted, for she really coveted one of the fine braids, but felt shy about asking the poor girl for even a part of her one beauty.

So July and August passed pleasantly and profitably to both girls, and in September they were to part. No more was said about poetry; and Emily soon became so interested in the busy, practical life about her that her own high-flown dreams were quite forgotten, and she learned to enjoy the sweet prose of daily labor.

One breezy afternoon as she and her mother sat resting from a stroll on the wayside bank among the goldenrod and asters, they saw Becky coming up the long hill with a basket on her arm. She walked slowly, as if lost in thought, yet never missed pushing aside with a decided gesture of her foot every stone that lay in her way. There were many in that rocky path, but Becky left it smoother as she climbed, and paused now and then to send some especially sharp or large one spinning into the grassy ditch beside the road.

"Isn't she a curious girl, Mamma? So tired after her long walk to town, yet so anxious not to leave a stone in the way," said Emily, as they watched her slow approach.

"A very interesting one to me, dear, because under that humble exterior lies a fine, strong character. It is like Becky to clear her way, even up a dusty hill where the first rain will wash out many more stones. Let us ask her why she does it. I've observed the habit before, and always meant to ask," replied Mrs. Spenser.

"Here we are! Come and rest a minute, Becky, and tell us if you mend roads as well as ever so many other things," called Emily, beckoning with a smile, as the girl looked up and saw them.

"Oh, it's a trick of mine; I caught it of Father when I was a little thing, and do it without knowing it half the time," said Becky, sinking down upon a mossy rock, as if rest were welcome.

"Why did he do it?" asked Emily, who knew that her friend loved to talk of her father.

"Well, it's a family failing I guess, for his father did the same, only *he* began with his farm and let the roads alone. The land used to be pretty much all rocks up here, you know, and farmers had to clear the ground if they wanted crops. It was a hard fight, and took a sight of time and patience to grub out roots and blast rocks and pick up stones that seemed to grow faster than anything else. But they kept on, and now see!"

As she spoke, Becky pointed proudly to the wide, smooth fields lying before them, newly shorn of grass or grain, waving with corn, or rich in garden crops ripening for winter stores. Here and there were rocky strips unreclaimed, as if to show what had been done; and massive stone walls surrounded pasture, field, and garden.

"A good lesson in patience and perseverance, my dear, and does great honor to the men who made the wilderness blossom like the rose," said Mrs. Spenser.

"Then you can't wonder that they loved it and we want to keep it. I guess it would break Mother's heart to sell this place, and we are all working as hard as ever we can to pay off the mortgage. Then we'll be just the happiest family in New Hampshire," said Becky, fondly surveying the old farmhouse, the rocky hill, and the precious fields won from the forest.

"You never need fear to lose it; we will see to that if you will let us," began Mrs. Spenser, who was both a rich and a generous woman.

"Oh, thank you! But we won't need help I guess; and if we should, Mrs. Taylor made us promise to come to her," cried Becky. "She found us just in our hardest time, and wanted to fix things then; but we are proud in our way, and Mother said she'd rather work it off if she could. Then what did that dear lady do but talk to the folks round here, and show 'em how a branch railroad down to Peeksville would increase the value of the land, and how good this valley would be for strawberries and asparagus and garden truck if we could only get it to market. Some of the rich men took up the plan, and we hope it will be done this fall. It will be the making of us, for our land is first-rate for small crops, and the children can help at that, and with a *deepot* close by, it would be such easy work. That's what I call helping folks to help themselves. Won't it be grand?"

Becky looked so enthusiastic that Emily could not remain uninterested, though market-gardening did not sound very romantic.

"I hope it will come, and next year we shall see you all hard at it. What a good woman Mrs. Taylor is!"

"Ain't she? And the sad part of it is, she can't do and enjoy all she wants to, because her health is so poor. She was a country girl, you know, and went to work in the city as waiter in a boardinghouse. A rich man fell in love with her and married her, and she took care of him for years, and he left her all his money. She was quite broken down, but she wanted to make his name loved and honored after his death, as he hadn't done any good while he lived; so she gives away heaps, and is never tired of helping poor folks and doing all sorts of grand things to make the world better. I call that splendid!"

"So do I, yet it is only what you are doing in a small way, Becky," said Mrs. Spenser, as the girl paused, out of breath. "Mrs. Taylor clears the stones out of people's paths, making their road easier to climb than hers has been, and leaving behind her fruitful fields for others to reap. This is a better work than making verses, for it is the real poetry of life, and brings to those who give themselves to it, no matter in what humble ways, something sweeter than fame and more enduring than fortune."

"So it does! I see that now, and know why we love Father as we do, and want to keep what he worked so hard to give us. He used to say every stone cleared away was just so much help to the boys; and he used to tell me his plans as I trotted after him round the farm, helping all I could, being the oldest, and like him, he said."

Becky paused with full eyes, for not even to these good friends could she ever tell the shifts and struggles in which she had bravely borne her part during the long hard years that had wrested the little homestead from the stony-hearted hills.

The musical chime of a distant clock reminded her that supper-time was near, and she sprang up as if much refreshed by this pleasant rest by the wayside. As she pulled out her handkerchief, a little roll of pale blue ribbon fell from her pocket, and Emily caught it up, exclaiming mischievously, "Are you going to make yourself fine next Sunday, when Moses Pennel calls, Becky?"

The girl laughed and blushed as she said, carefully folding up the ribbon:

"I'm going to do something with it that I like a sight better than that. Poor Moses won't come any more, I guess. I'm not going to leave Mother till the girls can take my place, and only then to teach, if I can get a good school somewhere near."

"We shall see!" and Emily nodded wisely.

"We shall!" and Becky nodded decidedly, as she trudged on up the steep hill beside Mrs. Spenser, while Emily walked slowly behind, poking every stone she saw into the grass, unmindful of the detriment to her delicate shoes, being absorbed in a new and charming idea of trying to follow Mrs. Taylor's example in a small way.

A week later the last night came, and just as they were parting for bed, in rushed one of the boys with the exciting news that the railroad surveyors were in town, the folks talking about the grand enterprise, and the fortune of the place made forever.

Great was the rejoicing in the old farmhouse; the boys cheered, the little girls danced, the two mothers dropped a happy tear as they shook each other's hands, and Emily embraced Becky, tenderly exclaiming, "There, you dear thing, is a great stone shoved out of *your* way, and a clear road to fortune at last; for I shall tell all my friends to buy your butter and eggs, and fruit and pigs, and everything you send to market on that blessed railroad."

"A keg of our best winter butter is going by stage express to-morrow anyway; and when our apples come, we shan't need a railroad to get 'em to you, my darling dear," answered Becky, holding the delicate girl in her arms with a look and gesture half sisterly, half motherly, wholly fond and grateful.

When Emily got to her room, she found that butter and apples were not all the humble souvenirs offered in return for many comfortable gifts to the whole family.

On the table, in a pretty birch-bark cover, lay several of Becky's best poems neatly copied, as Emily had expressed a wish to keep them; and round the rustic volume, like a ring of red gold, lay a great braid of Becky's hair, tied with the pale blue ribbon she had walked four miles to buy, that her present might look its best.

Of course there were more embraces and kisses, and thanks and loving words, before Emily at last lulled herself to sleep planning a Christmas box, which should supply every wish and want of the entire family if she could find them out.

Next morning they parted; but these were not mere summer friends, and they did not lose sight of one another, though their ways lay far apart. Emily had found a new luxury to bring more pleasure into life, a new medicine to strengthen soul and body; and in helping others, she helped herself wonderfully.

Becky went steadily on her dutiful way, till the homestead was free, the lads able to work the farm alone, the girls old enough to fill her place, and the good mother willing to rest at last among her children. Then Becky gave herself to teaching — a noble task, for which she was well fitted, and in which she found both profit and pleasure, as she led her flock along the paths from which she removed the stumbling-blocks for their feet, as well as for her own. She put her poetry into her life, and made of it "a grand sweet song" in which beauty and duty rhymed so well that the country girl became a more useful, beloved, and honored woman than if she had tried to sing for fame which never satisfies.

So each symbolical plant stood in its own place, and lived its appointed life. The delicate fern grew in the conservatory among tea-roses and camelias, adding grace to every bouquet of which it formed a part, whether it faded in a ballroom, or was carefully cherished by some poor invalid's bedside — a frail thing, yet with tenacious roots and strong stem, nourished by memories of the rocky nook where it had learned its lesson so well. The mountain laurel clung to the bleak hillside, careless of wintry wind and snow, as its sturdy branches spread year by year, with its ever-green leaves for Christmas cheer, its rosy flowers for springtime, its fresh beauty free to all as it clothed the wild valley with a charm that made a little poem of the lovely spot where the pines whispered, woodbirds sang, and the hidden brook told the sweet message it brought from the mountaintop where it was born.

CORNY'S CATAMOUNT

from *Spinning Wheel Stories*, 1884

Catamount was the old-fashioned name for the ordinary New England wildcat or bobcat, a rough-coated, stout-legged gray creature which an enterprising dog can still find in the New England woods and chase up the nearest tree, the cat spitting ferociously. A boy like Corny, seeing himself in fancy as hero of a forest adventure, could very well have set out in all his cheerful ignorance, to pit his wits against this elusive and often savage beast of which he had heard so many stories.

CORNY'S CATAMOUNT

Two boys sat on the bars, one whittling, the other whistling — not for want of thought by any means, for his brow was knit in an anxious frown, and he paused now and then to thump the rail with an impatient exclamation. The other lad appeared to be absorbed in shaping an arrow from the slender stick in his hand, but he watched his neighbor with a grin, saying a few words occasionally which seemed to add to his irritation, though they were in a sympathizing tone.

"Oh, well, if a chap can't do a thing he can't; and he'd better give up and say, 'Beat.' "

"But I won't give up, and I never say 'Beat.' I'm not going to be laughed out of it, and I'll do what I said I would, if it takes all summer, Chris Warner."

"You'll have to be pretty spry, then, for there's only two more days to August," replied the whittler, shutting one eye to look along his arrow and see if it was true.

"I intend to be spry, and if you won't go and blab, I'll tell you a plan I made last night."

"Guess you can trust me. I've heard about a dozen plans now, and never told one of 'em."

"They all failed, so there was nothing to tell. But this one is *not* going to fail, if I die for it. I feel that it's best to tell someone, because it is really dangerous; and if anything *should* happen to me, as is very likely, it would save time and trouble."

"Don't seem to feel anxious a mite. But I'll stand ready to pick up the pieces, if you come to grief."

"Now, Chris, it's mean of you to keep on making fun when I'm in dead earnest; and this may be the last thing you can do for me."

"Wait till I get out my handkerchief; if you're going to be affectin' I may want it. Granite's cheap up here; just mention what you'd like on your tombstone and I'll see that it's done, if it takes my last cent."

The big boy in the blue overalls spoke with such a comical drawl that the slender city lad could not help laughing, and with a slap that nearly sent his neighbor off his perch, Corny said good-naturedly:

"Come now, stop joking and lend a hand, and I'll do anything I can for you. I've set my heart on shooting a wildcat, and I know I can if I once get a good chance. Mother won't let me go off far enough, so of course I don't do it, and then you all jeer at me. Tomorrow we are going up the mountain, and I'm set on trying again, for Abner says the big woods are the place to find the 'varmint.' Now you hold your tongue, and let me slip away when I think we've hit the right spot. I'm not a bit afraid, and while the rest go joking to the top, I'll plunge into the woods and see what I can do."

"All right. Better take old Buff; he'll bring you home when you get lost, and keep puss from clawing you. You won't like that part of the fun as much as you expect to, maybe," said Chris, with a sly twinkle of the eye, as he glanced at Corny and then away to the vast forest that stretched far up the mighty mountain's side.

"No, I don't want any help, and Buff will betray me by barking; I prefer to go alone. I shall take some lunch and plenty of shot, and have a glorious time, even if I don't meet that confounded beast. I will keep dashing in and out of the woods as we go; then no one will miss me for a while, and when they do you just say, 'Oh, he's all right; he'll be along directly,' and go ahead, and let me alone."

Corny spoke so confidently, and looked so pleased with his plan, that honest Chris could not bear to tell him how much danger he would run in that pathless forest, where older hunters than he had been lost.

"Don't feel as if I cared to tell any lies about it, and I don't advise your goin'; but if you're mad for catamounts, I s'pose I must humor you and say nothing. Only bear in mind, Abner and I will be along, and if you get into a scrape jest give a yell and we'll come."

"No fear of that; I've tramped around all summer, and know my way like an Indian. Keep the girls quiet, and let me have a good lark. I'll turn up all right by sundown; so don't worry. Not a word to Mother, mind, or she won't let me go. I'll make things straight with her after the fun is over."

"That ain't just square; but it's not my funeral, so I won't meddle. Hope you'll have first-rate sport, and bag a brace of cats. One thing you mind, don't get too nigh before you fire; and keep out of sight of the critters as much as you can."

Chris spoke in a deep whisper, looking so excited and impressed by the reckless courage of his mate that Corny felt himself a Leatherstocking, and went off to tea with his finger on his lips, full of boyish faith in his own powers. If he had seen Chris dart behind the barn, and there roll upon the grass in convulsions of laughter, he would have been both surprised and hurt.

No deacon could have been more sober, however, than Chris when they met next morning, while the party of summer boarders at the old farmhouse were in a pleasant bustle of preparation for the long-expected day on the mountain. Three merry girls, a pair of small boys, two amiable mammas, Chris and Corny, made up the party, with Abner to drive the big wagon drawn by Milk and Molasses, the yellow span.

"All aboard!" shouted our young Nimrod, in a hurry to be off, as the lunch-basket was handed up, and the small boys packed in the most uncomfortable corners, regardless of their arms and legs.

Away they rattled with a parting cheer, and peace fell upon the farmhouse for a few hours, to the great contentment of the good people left behind. Corny's mother was one of them, and her last words were — "A pleasant day, dear. I wish you'd leave that gun at home; I'm so afraid you'll get hurt with it."

"No fun without it. Don't worry, Mammy; I'm old enough to take care of myself."

"I'll see to him, ma'am," called Chris, as he hung on behind, and waved his old straw hat, with a steady, reliable sort of look, that made the anxious lady feel more comfortable.

"We are going to walk up, and leave the horses to rest; so I can choose my time. See, I've got a bottle of cold tea in this pocket, and a lot of grub in the other. No danger of my starving, is there?" whispered Corny, as he leaned over to Chris, who sat, apparently, on nothing, with his long legs dangling into space.

"Shouldn't wonder if you needed every mite of it. Hunting is mighty hard work on a hot day, and this is going to be a blazer," answered Chris, pulling his big straw hat lower over his eyes.

As we intend to follow Corny's adventures, we need not pause to describe the drive, which was a merry one; with girls chattering, mammas holding on to excited small boys, in danger of flying out at every jolt, Abner joking till everyone roared, Corny's dangerous evolutions with the beloved gun, and the gymnastic feats Chris performed, jumping off to pick flowers for the ladies, and getting on again while Milk and Molasses tore up and down the rough road as if they enjoyed it.

About ten o'clock they reached the foot of the mountain; and after a short rest at the hotel, began the three-mile ascent in high spirits. Abner was to follow later with the wagon, to bring the party down; so Chris was guide, as he knew the way well, and often came with people. The girls and younger boys hurried on, full of eagerness to reach the top. The ladies went more slowly, enjoying the grand beauty of the scene, while Chris carried the lunch-basket, and Corny lingered in the rear, waiting for a good chance to "plunge."

He wanted to be off before Abner came, as he well knew that wise man and mighty hunter would never let him go alone.

"The very next path I see, I'll dive in and run; Chris can't leave the rest to follow, and if I once get a good start, they won't catch me in a hurry," thought the boy, longing to be free and alone in the wild woods that tempted him on either hand.

Just as he was tightening his belt to be ready for the run, Mrs. Barker, the stout lady, called him; and being a well-bred lad, he hastened at once to see what she wanted, feeling that he was the only gentleman in the party.

"Give me your arm, dear; I'm getting very tired, and fear I can't hold out to the top, without a little help," said the poor lady, red and panting with the heat, and steepness of the road.

"Certainly, ma'am," answered Corny, obeying at once, and inwardly resolving to deposit his fair burden on the first fallen log they came to, and make his escape.

But Mrs. Barker got on bravely, with the support of his strong arm, and chatted away so delightfully that Corny would really have enjoyed the walk, if his soul had not been yearning for catamounts. He did his best, but when they passed opening after opening into the green recesses of the wood, and the granite boulders grew more and more plentiful, his patience gave out, and he began to plan what he could say to excuse himself. Chris was behind, apparently deaf and blind to his calls and imploring glances, though he grinned cheerfully when poor Corny looked round and beckoned, as well as he could, with a gun on one arm and a stout lady on the other.

"The hardest part is coming now, and we'd better rest a moment. Here's a nice rock, and the last spring we are likely to see till we get to the top. Come on Chris, and give us the dipper. Mrs. Barker wants a drink, and so do I," called the young hunter, driven to despair at last.

Up came Chris, and while he rummaged in the well-packed basket, Corny slipped into the wood, leaving the good lady with her thanks half spoken, sitting on a warm stone beside a muddy little pool. A loud laugh followed him, as he scrambled through the tall ferns and went plunging down the steep mountainside, eager to reach the lower woods.

"Let him laugh; it will be my turn when I go home, with a fine cat over my shoulder," thought Corny, tearing along, heedless of falls, scratches, and bruised knees.

At length he paused for breath, and looked about him well satisfied, for the spot was lonely and lovely enough to suit any hunter. The tallest pines he ever saw sighed far overhead; the ground was ankle deep in moss, and gay with scarlet bunch-berries; every fallen log was veiled by sweet-scented Linnea, green vines or nodding brakes; while hidden brooks sang musically, and the air was full of the soft flutter of leaves, the whir of wings, the sound of birds gossiping sweetly in the safe shelter of the forest, where human feet so seldom came.

"I'll rest a bit, and then go along down, keeping a look out for puss by the way," thought Corny, feeling safe and free, and very happy, for he had his own way, at last, and a whole day to lead the life he loved.

So he bathed his hot face, took a cool drink, and lay on the moss, staring up into the green gloom of the pines, blissfully dreaming of the joys of a hunter's life — till a peculiar cry startled him to his feet, and sent him creeping warily toward the sound. Whether it was a new kind of bird, or a fox, or a bear, he did not know, but fondly hoped it was a wildcat; though he was well aware that the latter creature sleeps by day, and prowls by night. Abner said they purred and snarled and gave a mewing sort of cry; but which it was now he could not tell, having unfortunately been half asleep.

On he went, looking up into the trees for a furry bunch, behind every log, and in every rocky hole, longing and hoping to discover his heart's desire. But a hawk was all he saw above, an ugly snake was the only living thing he found among the logs, and a fat woodchuck's hind legs vanished down the most attractive hole. He shot at all three and missed them, so pushed on, pretending that he did not care for such small game.

"Now this is what I call fun," he said to himself, tramping gaily along, and at that moment went splash into a mud-hole concealed under the grass. He sank up to his knees, and with great difficulty got out by clinging to the tussocks that grew near. In his struggles the lunch was lost, for the bottle broke and the pocket where the sandwiches were stored was full of mud. A woeful spectacle was the trim lad as he emerged from the slough, black and dripping in front, well spattered behind, hatless, and one shoe gone, having been carelessly left unlaced in the ardor of the chase.

"Here's a mess!" thought poor Corny, surveying himself with great disgust and feeling very helpless, as well as tired, hungry, and mad. "Luckily, my powder is dry and my gun safe; so my fun isn't spoiled, though I do look like a wallowing pig. I've heard of mud baths, but I never took one before, and I'll be shot if I do again."

So he washed as well as he could, hoping the sun would dry him, picked out a few bits of bread unspoiled by the general wreck, and trudged on with less ardor, though by no means discouraged yet.

"I'm too high for any game but birds, and those I don't want. I'll go slap down, and come out in the valley. Abner said any brook would show the way, and this rascal that led me into a scrape shall lead me out," he said, as he followed the little stream that went tumbling over the stones, that increased as the ground sloped toward the deep ravine, where a waterfall shone like silver in the sun.

"I'll take a bath if the pool is big enough, and that will set me up. Shouldn't wonder if I'd got poisoned a bit with some of these vines I've been tearing through. My hands smart like fury, and I guess the mosquitoes have about eaten my face up. Never saw such clouds of stingers before," said Corny, looking at his scratched hands, and rubbing his hot face in great discomfort — for it was the gnat that drove the lion mad, you remember.

It was easy to say, "I'll follow the brook," but not so easy to do it; for the frolicsome stream went headlong over rocks, crept under fallen logs, and now and then hid itself so cleverly that one had to look and listen carefully to recover the trail. It was long past noon when Corny came out near the waterfall, so tired and hungry that he heartily wished himself back among the party, who had lunched well and were now probably driving gaily homeward to a good supper.

No chance for a bath appeared, so he washed his burning face and took a rest, enjoying the splendid view far over valley and intervale through the gap in the mountain range. He was desperately tired with these hours of rough travel, and very hungry; but would not own it, and sat considering what to do next, for he saw by the sun that the afternoon was half over. There was time to go back the way he had come, and by following the path down the hill he could reach the hotel and get supper and a bed, or be driven home. That was the wise thing to do, but his pride rebelled against returning empty-handed after all his plans and boasts of great exploits.

"I won't go home, to be laughed at by Chris and Abner. I'll shoot something, if I stay all night. Who cares for hunger and mosquito bites? Not I. Hunters can bear more than that, I guess. The next live thing I see I'll shoot it, and make a fire and have a jolly supper. Now which way shall I go — up or down? A pretty hard prospect, either way."

The sight of an eagle soaring above him seemed to answer his question, and fill him with new strength and ardor. To shoot the king of birds and take him home in triumph would cover the hunter with glory. It should be done! And away he went, climbing, tumbling, leaping from rock to rock, toward the place where the eagle had alighted. More cuts and bruises, more vain shots, and all the reward of his eager struggles was a single feather that floated down as the great bird soared serenely away, leaving the boy exhausted and disappointed in a wilderness of granite boulders, with no sign of a path to show the way out.

As he leaned breathless and weary against the crag where he had fondly hoped to find the eagle's nest, he realized for the first time what a foolhardy thing he had done. Here he was, alone, without a guide, in this wild region where there was neither food nor shelter, and night coming on. Utterly used up, he could not get home now if he had known the way; and suddenly all the tales he had ever heard of men lost in the mountains came into his head. If he had not been weak with hunger he would have felt better able to bear it; but his legs trembled under him, his head ached with the glare of the sun, and a queer faintness came over him now and then; for the city lad was unused to such violent exercise, plucky as he was.

"The only thing to do now is to get down to the valley, if I can, before dark. Abner said there was an old cabin, where the hunters used to sleep, somewhere round that way. I can try for it, and perhaps shoot something on the way. May break my bones, but I can't sit and starve up here, and I was a fool to come. I'll keep the feather anyway, to prove that I really saw an eagle; that's better than nothing."

Still bravely trying to affect the indifference to danger and fatigue which hunters are always described as possessing in such a remarkable degree, Corny slung the useless gun on his back and began the steep descent, discovering now the perils he had been too eager to see before. He was a good climber, but was stiff with weariness, and his hands already sore with scratches and poison; so he went slowly, feeling quite unfit for such hard work. Coming to the ravine, he found the only road was down its precipitous side to the valley, that looked so safe and pleasant now. Stunted pines grew in the fissures of the rocks, and their strong roots helped the clinging hands and feet as the boy painfully climbed, slipped, and swung along, fearing every minute to come to some impassable barrier in the dangerous path.

But he got on wonderfully well, and was feeling much encouraged, when his foot slipped, the root he held gave way, and down he went, rolling and bumping to his death on the rocks below, he thought, as a crash came, and he knew no more.

"Wonder if I'm dead?" was the first idea that occurred to him as he opened his eyes and saw a brilliant sky above him, all purple, gold, and red.

He seemed floating in the air, for he swayed to and fro on a soft bed, a pleasant murmur reached his ear, and when he looked down he saw what looked like clouds, misty and white, below him. He lay a few minutes drowsily musing, for the fall had stunned him; then, as he moved his hand something pricked it, and he felt pine needles in the fingers that closed over them.

"Caught in a tree, by Jupiter!" and all visions of heaven vanished in a breath, as he sat up and stared about him, wide awake now, and conscious of many aching bones.

Yes, there he lay among the branches of one of the sturdy pines, into which he had fallen on his way down the precipice. Blessed little tree! set there to save a life, and teach a lesson to a willful young heart that never forgot that hour.

Holding fast, lest a rash motion should set him bounding further down, like a living ball, Corney took an observation as rapidly as possible, for the red light was fading, and the mist rising from the valley. All he could see was a narrow ledge where the tree stood, and anxious to reach a safer bed for the night, he climbed cautiously down to drop on the rock, so full of gratitude for safety that he could only lie quite still for a little while, thinking of Mother, and trying not to cry.

He was much shaken by the fall, his flesh bruised, his clothes torn, and his spirit cowed; for hunger, weariness, pain, and danger showed him what a very feeble creature he was, after all. He could do no more till morning, and resigned himself to a night on the mountainside, glad to be there alive, though doubtful what daylight would show him. Too tired to move, he lay watching the western sky, where the sun set gloriously behind the purple hills. All below was wrapped in mist, and not a sound reached him but the sigh of the pine, and the murmur of the waterfall.

"This is a first-class scrape. What a fool I was not to go back when I could, instead of blundering down here where no one can get at me, and as like as not I can't get out alone! Gun smashed in that confounded fall, so I can't even fire a shot to call help. Nothing to eat or drink, and very likely a day or so to spend here till I'm found, if I ever am. Chris said, 'Yell, if you want us.' Much good that would do now! I'll try, though." And getting up on his weary legs, Corny shouted till he was hoarse; but echo alone answered him, and after a few efforts he gave it up, trying to accept the situation like a man. As if kind Nature took pity on the poor boy, the little ledge was soft with lichens and thin grass, and here and there grew a sprig of checkerberry, sown by the wind, sheltered by the tree, and nourished by the moisture that trickled down the rock from some hidden spring. Eagerly Corny ate the sweet leaves to stay the pangs of hunger that gnawed him, and finished his meal with grass and pine needles, calling himself a calf, and wishing his pasture were wider.

"The fellows we read about always come to grief in a place where they can shoot a bird, catch a fish, or knock over some handy beast for supper," he said, talking to himself for company. "Even the old chap lost in the bush in Australia had a savage with him who dug a hole in a tree, and pulled out a nice fat worm to eat. I'm not lucky enough even to find a sassafras bush to chew, or a bird's egg to suck. My poor gun is broken, or I might bang away at a hawk, and cook him for supper, if the bog didn't spoil my matches as it did my lunch. Oh, well! I'll pull through, I guess, and when it's all over, it will be a jolly good story to tell."

Then, hoping to forget his woes in sleep, he nestled under the low-growing branches of the pine, and lay blinking drowsily at the twilight world outside. A dream came, and he saw the old farm-house in sad confusion, caused by his absence — the women cry-ing, the men sober, all anxious, and all making ready to come and look for him. So vivid was it that he woke himself by crying out, "Here I am!" and nearly went over the ledge, stretching out his arms to Abner.

The start and the scare made it hard to go to sleep again, and he sat looking at the solemn sky, full of stars that seemed watching over him alone there, like a poor, lost child on the great mountain's stony breast. He had never seen the world at that hour before, and it made a deep impression on him; for it was a vast, wild scene, full of gloomy shadows below, unknown dangers around, and a new sense of utter littleness and helplessness, which taught the boy human dependence upon Heavenly love as no words, even from his mother's tender lips, could have done. Thoughts of the suffering his willfulness had given her wrung a few penitent tears from him, which he was not ashamed to shed, since only the kind stars saw them, and better still, he resolved to own the fault, to atone for it, and to learn wisdom from this lesson, which might yet prove to be a very bitter one.

He felt better after this little breakdown, and presently his thoughts were turned from conscience to catamounts again; for sounds in the woods below led him to believe that the much-desired animal was on the prowl. His excited fancy painted dozens of them not far away, waiting to be shot, and there he was, cooped up on that narrow ledge, with a broken gun, unable even to get a look at them. He felt that it was a just punishment, and after the first regret tried to comfort himself with the fact that he was much safer where he was than alone in the forest at that hour, for vari-ous nocturnal voices suggested restless and dangerous neighbors.

Presently his wakeful eyes saw lights twinkling far off on the opposite side of the ravine, and he imagined he heard shouts and shots. But the splash of the waterfall and the rush of the night wind deadened the sounds to his ear, and drowned his own reply.

"They are looking for me, and will never think of this strange place. I can't make them hear, and must wait till morning. Poor Chris will get an awful scolding for letting me go. Don't believe he told a word till he had to. I'll make it up to him. Chris is a capital fellow, and I just wish I had him here to make things jolly," thought the lonely lad.

But soon the lights vanished, the sounds died away, and the silence of midnight brooded over the hills, seldom broken except by the soft cry of an owl, the rustle of the pine, or a louder gust of wind as it grew strong and cold. Corny kept awake as long as he could, fearing to dream and fall; but by and by he dropped off, and slept soundly till the chill of dawn waked him.

At any other time he would have heartily enjoyed the splendor of the eastern sky, as the red glow spread and brightened, till the sun came dazzling through the gorge, making the wild solitude beautiful and grand.

Now, however, he would have given it all for a hot beefsteak and a cup of coffee, as he wet his lips with a few drops of ice-cold water, and browsed over his small pasture till not a green spire remained. He was stiff, and full of pain, but daylight and the hope of escape cheered him up, and gave him coolness and courage to see how best he could accomplish his end.

The wind soon blew away the mist and let him see that the dry bed of a stream lay just below. To reach it he must leap, at risk of his bones, or find some means to swing down ten or twelve feet. Once there, it was pretty certain that by following the rough road he would come into the valley, from whence he could easily find his way home. Much elated at this unexpected good fortune, he took the strap that had slung his gun, the leathern belt about his waist, and the strong cords of his pouch, and knotting them together, made a rope long enough to let him drop within two or three feet of the stones below. This he fastened firmly round the trunk of the pine, and finished his preparations by tying his handkerchief to one of the branches, that it might serve as a guide for him, a signal for others, and a trophy of his grand fall.

Then, putting a little sprig of the evergreen tree in his jacket, with a grateful thought of all it had done for him, he swung himself off and landed safely below, not minding a few extra bumps after his late exploits at tumbling.

Feeling like a prisoner set free, he hurried as fast as bare feet and stiff legs would carry him along the bed of the stream, coming at last into the welcome shelter of the woods, which seemed more beautiful than ever, after the bleak region of granite in which he had been all night.

Anxious to report himself alive, and relieve his mother's anxiety, he pressed on till he struck the path, and soon saw, not far away, the old cabin Abner had spoken of. Just before this happy moment he had heard a shot fired somewhere in the forest, and as he hurried toward the sound he saw an animal dart into the hut, as if for shelter.

Whether it was a rabbit, woodchuck or dog, he had not seen, as a turn in the path prevented a clear view; and hoping it was old Buff looking for him, he ran in, to find himself face to face with a catamount at last.

There she was, the big, fierce cat, crouched in a corner, with fiery eyes, growling and spitting at sight of an enemy, but too badly wounded to fight, as the blood that dripped from her neck and the tremble of her limbs plainly showed.

"Now's my chance! Don't care who shot her, I'll kill her, and have her too, if I pay my last dollar," thought Corny; and catching up a stout bit of timber fallen from the old roof, he struck one quick blow, which finished poor puss, who gave up the ghost with a savage snarl, and a vain effort to pounce on him.

This splendid piece of good luck atoned for all the boy had gone through, and only waiting to be sure the beast was quite dead and past clawing, he flung his prize over his shoulder, and with re-

newed strength and spirit trudged along the woodland road toward home, proudly imagining his triumphal entry upon the scene
of suspense and alarm.

"Wish I didn't look so like a scarecrow; but perhaps my rags
will add to the effect. Won't the girls laugh at my swelled face,
and scream at the cat. Poor Mammy will mourn over me and
coddle me up as if I'd been to the wars. Hope some house isn't very
far off, for I don't believe I can lug this brute much farther, I'm so
starved and shaky."

Just as he paused to take breath and shift his burden from one
shoulder to the other, a loud shout startled him, and a moment
after, several men came bursting through the wood, cheering like
lunatics as they approached.

It was Abner, Chris, and some of the neighbors, setting out
again on their search, after a night of vain wandering. Corny
could have hugged them all and cried like a girl; but pride kept
him steady, though his faced showed his joy as he nodded his hatless head with a cool:

"Hullo!"

Chris burst into his ringing laugh, and danced a wild sort of jig
round his mate, as the only way in which he could fitly express his
relief; for he had been so bowed down with remorse at his impru-
dence in letting Corny go that no one could find the heart to blame
him, and all night the poor lad had rushed up and down seeking,
calling, hoping, and fearing, till he was about used up, and looked
nearly as dilapidated as Corny.

The tale was soon told, and received with the most flattering
signs of interest, wonder, sympathy, and admiration.

"Why in thunder didn't you tell me? And I'd a got up a hunt
wuth havin' — not go stramashing off alone on a wild-goose chase
like this. Never did see such a chap as you be for gittin' inter
scrapes — and out of 'em, too, I'm bound to own," growled Abner.

"That isn't a wild goose, is it?" proudly demanded Corny,

pointing to the cat, which now lay on the ground, while he leaned against a tree to hide his weariness; for he felt ready to drop, now all the excitement was over.

"No it ain't, and I congratulate you on a good job. Where did you shoot her?" asked Abner, stooping to examine the creature.

"Didn't shoot her; broke my gun when I took that header down the mountain. I hit her a rap with a club, in the cabin where I found her," answered Corny, heartily wishing he need not share the prize with anyone. But he was honest, and added at once, "Someone else had put a bullet into her; I only finished her off."

"Chris did it; he fired a spell back and see the critter run, but we was too keen after you to stop for any other game. Guess you've had enough of catamounts for one spell, hey?" And Abner laughed as he looked at poor Corny, who was a more sorry spectacle than he knew — ragged and rough, hatless and shoeless, his face red and swelled with the poisoning and bites, his eyes heavy with weariness, and in his mouth a bit of wild-cherry bark which he chewed ravenously.

"No, I haven't! I want this one, and will buy it if Chris will let me. I said I'd kill one, and I did, and want to keep the skin; for I ought to have something to show after all this knocking about and turning somersaults half a mile long," answered Corny stoutly, as he tried to shoulder his load again.

"Here, give me the varmint, and you hang on to Chris, my boy, or we'll have to cart you home. You've done first-rate, and now you want a good meal of vittles to set you up. Right about face, neighbors, and home we go, to the tune of Hail Columby."

As Abner spoke, the procession set forth. The tall, jolly man, with the dead animal at his back, went first; then Corny, trying not to lean on the arm Chris put round him, but very glad of the support; next the good farmers, all talking at once; while old Buff soberly brought up the rear, with his eye on the wildcat, well knowing that he would have a fine feast when the handsome skin was off.

In this order they reached home, and Corny tumbled into his mother's arms, to be no more seen for some hours. What went on in her room, no one knows; but when at last the hero emerged, refreshed by sleep and food, clad in clean clothes, his wounds bound up, and plantain leaves dipped in cream spread upon his afflicted countenance, he received the praises and congratulations showered upon him very meekly. He made no more boasts of skill and courage that summer, set out on no more wild hunts, and gave up his own wishes so cheerfully that it was evident something had worked a helpful change in willful Corny.

He liked to tell the story of that day and night when his friends were recounting adventures by sea and land; but he never said much about the hours on the ledge, always owned that Chris shot the beast, and usually ended by sagely advising his hearers to let their mothers know when they went off on a lark of that kind. Those who knew and loved him best observed that he was fonder than ever of nibbling checkerberry leaves, that he didn't mind being laughed at for liking to wear a bit of pine in his buttonhole, and that the skin of the catamount so hardly won lay before his study table till the moths ate it up.

WATER LILIES

from *A Garland for Girls*, 1886

*Quite early in her journals Louisa speaks of a visit to Mt. Desert
and of the pleasure she feels at being near the sea. She was often
at the seashore later and finally, in her prosperous days, she
bought a house at Nonquit, Massachusetts, largely for the benefit
of little Louisa Neiriker. The background of this story sounds
much like a return in fancy to Mt. Desert with its great storm-
beaten rocks, its lighthouses and summer-resort population.*

WATER LILIES

A party of people, young and old, sat on the piazza of a seaside hotel one summer morning, discussing plans for the day as they waited for the mail.

"Hullo! Here comes Christie Johnstone," exclaimed one of the young men perched on the railing, who was poisoning the fresh air with the sickly scent of a cigarette.

"So 'tis, with 'Flucker, the baddish boy' in tow, as large as life," added another, with a pleasant laugh as he turned to look.

The newcomers certainly looked somewhat like Charles Reade's picturesque pair, and everyone watched them with idle interest as they drew nearer. A tall, robust girl of seventeen, with dark eyes and hair, a fine color on her brown cheek, and vigor in every movement, came up the rocky path from the beach with a basket of lobsters on one arm, of fish on the other, and a wicker tray of water lilies on her head. The scarlet and silver of the fish contrasted prettily with the dark blue of her rough dress, and the pile of water flowers made a fitting crown for this bonny young fish-wife. A sturdy lad of twelve came lurching after her in a pair of very large rubber boots, with a dilapidated straw hat on the back of his head and a pail on either arm.

Straight on went the girl, never turning head or eyes as she passed the group on the piazza and vanished round the corner, though it was evident that she heard the laugh the last speech produced, for the color deepened in her cheeks and her step quickened. The boy, however, returned the glances bent upon him, and

answered the smiles with such a cheerful grin that the youth with
the cigarette called out:

"Good morning, Skipper! Where do you hail from?"

"Island, yender," answered the boy, with a gesture of his thumb
over his shoulder.

"Oh, you are the lighthouse-keeper, are you?"

"No, I ain't; me and Gramper's fishermen now."

"Your name is Flucker Johnstone, and your sister's Christie, I
think?" added the youth, enjoying the amusement of the young
ladies about him.

"It's Sammy Bowen, and hern's Ruth."

"Have you got a Boaz over there for her?"

"No, we've got a devilfish, a real whacker."

This unexpected reply produced a roar from the gentlemen,
while the boy grinned good-naturedly, though without the least
idea what the joke was. Pretty Miss Ellery, who had been told that
she had "a rippling laugh," rippled sweetly as she leaned over the
railing to ask:

"Are those lilies in your pails? I want some if they are for sale."

"Sister'll fetch 'em round when she's left the lobs. I ain't got
none; this is bait for them fellers." And as if reminded of business
by the yells of several boys who had just caught sight of him,
Sammy abruptly weighed anchor and ran before the wind toward
the stable.

"Funny lot, these natives! Act as if they owned the place, and
are as stupid as their own fish," said the youth in the white yacht-
ing-suit, as he flung away his cigarette end.

"Don't agree with you, Fred. I've known people of this sort all
my life, and a finer set of honest, hard-working, independent men I
never met — brave as lions and tender as women in spite of their
rough ways," answered the other young man, who wore blue flan-
nel and had a gold band on his cap.

"Sailors and soldiers always stand by one another; so of course
you see the best side of these fellows, Captain. The girls are fine

creatures, I grant you; but their good looks don't last long, more's the pity!"

"Few women's would with the life they lead, so full of hard work, suspense, and sorrow. No one knows till one is tried, how much courage and faith it takes to keep young and happy when the men one loves are on the great sea," said a quiet, gray-haired lady, as she laid her hand on the knee of the young man in blue with a look that made him smile affectionately at her, with his own brown hands on hers.

"Shouldn't wonder if Ben Bowen was laid up, since the girl brings the fish. He's a fine old fellow. I've been to No Man's Land many a time blue-fishing with him; must ask after him," said an elderly gentleman who was pacing to and fro yearning for the morning papers.

"We might go over to the island and have a chowder-party or a fish-fry some moonlight night. I haven't been here for several years, but it used to be great fun, and I suppose we can do it now," suggested Miss Ellery with the laugh.

"By Jove, we will! And look up Christie; ask her when she comes round," said Mr. Fred, the youthful dude, untwining his languid legs as if the prospect put a little life into him.

"Of course we pay for any trouble we give; these people will do anything for money," began Miss Ellery; but Captain John, as they called the sailor, held up his hand with a warning, "Hush! She's coming," as Ruth's weather-beaten brown hat turned the corner.

She paused a moment to drop the empty baskets, shake her skirts, and put up a black braid that had fallen down; then, with the air of one resolved to do a distasteful task as quickly as possible, she came up the steps, held out the rough basket-cover, and said in a clear voice:

"Would any of the ladies like some fresh lilies? Ten cents a bunch."

A murmur from the ladies expressed their admiration of the

beautiful flowers, and the gentlemen pressed forward to buy and present every bunch with gallant haste. Ruth's eyes shone as the money fell into her hand, and several voices begged her to bring more lilies while they lasted.

"I didn't know the darlings would grow in salt water," said Miss Ellery, as she fondly gazed upon the cluster Mr. Fred had just offered her.

"They don't. There's a little fresh-water pond on our island, and they grow there — only place for miles around"; and Ruth looked at the delicate girl in ruffled white lawn and a mull hat, with a glance of mingled pity for her ignorance and admiration for her beauty.

"How silly of me! I am *such* a goose"; and Miss Ellery gurgled as she hid her face behind her red parasol.

"Ask about the fish-fry," whispered Mr. Fred, putting his head behind the rosy screen to assure the pretty creature that he didn't know any better himself.

"Oh yes, I will!" and, quite consoled, Miss Ellery called out, "Girl, will you tell me if we can have chowder-parties on your rocks as we used to a few seasons ago?"

"If you bring your own fish. Grandpa is sick and can't get 'em for you."

"We will provide them, but who will cook them for us? It's such horrid work."

"Anyone can fry fish! I will if you want me to," and Ruth half smiled, remembering that this girl who shuddered at the idea of pork and a hot frying-pan, used to eat as heartily as anyone when the crisp brown cunners were served up.

"Very good; then we'll engage you as cook, and come over to-night if it's clear and our fishing prospers. Don't forget a dozen of the finest lilies for this lady tomorrow morning. Pay you now, may not be up"; and Mr. Fred dropped a bright silver dollar into the basket with a patronizing air, intended to impress this rather too independent young person with a proper sense of inferiority.

Ruth quietly shook the money out upon the doormat, and said with a sudden sparkle in her black eyes:

"It's doubtful if I bring any more. Better wait till I do."

"I'm sorry your grandfather is sick. I'll come over and see him by and by, and bring the papers if he would like some," said the elderly gentleman as he came up with a friendly nod and real interest in his face.

"Very much, thank you, sir. He is very feeble now." And Ruth turned with a bright smile to welcome kind Mr. Wallace, who had not forgotten the old man.

"Christie has got a nice little temper of her own, and don't know how to treat a fellow when he wants to do her a favor," growled Mr. Fred, pocketing his dollar with a disgusted air.

"She appears to know how to treat a gentleman when *he* offers one," answered Blue Jacket, with a twinkle of the eye as if he enjoyed the other's discomfiture.

"Girls of that class always put on airs if they are the least bit pretty — so absurd!" said Miss Ellery, pulling up her long gloves as she glanced at the brown arms of the fisher-maiden.

"Girls of any class like to be treated with respect. Modesty in linsey-woolsey is as sweet as in muslin, my dear, and should be even more admired, according to my old-fashioned way of thinking," said the gray-haired lady.

"Hear! hear!" murmured her sailor nephew with an approving nod.

It was evident that Ruth had heard also, as she turned to go, for with a quick gesture she pulled three great lilies from her hat and laid them on the old lady's lap, saying with a grateful look, "Thank you, ma'am."

She had seen Miss Scott hand her bunch to a meek little governess who had been forgotten, and this was all she had to offer in return for the kindness which is so sweet to poor girls whose sensitive pride gets often wounded by trifles like these.

She was going without her baskets when Captain John swung

himself over the railing, and ran after her with them. He touched
his cap as he met her, and was thanked with as bright a smile as
that the elder gentleman had received; for his respectful "Miss
Bowen" pleased her much after the rude "Girl!" and the money
tossed to her as if she were a beggar. When he came back the mail
had arrived, and all scattered at once — Mr. Fred to spend the
dollar in more cigarettes, and Captain John to settle carefully in
his buttonhole the water lily Aunt Mary gave him, before both
young men went off to play tennis as if their bread depended on
it.

As it bid fair to be a moonlight night, the party of a dozen
young people, with Miss Scott and Mr. Wallace to act as matron
and admiral of the fleet, set off to the Island about sunset. Fish in
abundance had been caught, and a picnic supper provided to be
eaten on the rocks when the proper time arrived. They found
Sammy, in a clean blue shirt and a hat less like a Feejee headpiece,
willing to do the honors of the Island, beaming like a freckled
young merman as he paddled out to pull up the boats.

"Fire's all ready for kindlin', and Ruth's slicin' the pertaters.
Hope them fish is cleaned?" he added with a face of deep anxiety;
for that weary task would fall to him if not already done, and the
thought desolated his boyish soul.

"All ready, Sam! Lend a hand with these baskets, and then
steer for the lighthouse; the ladies want to see that first," answered
Captain John, as he tossed a stray cookie into Sammy's mouth
with a smile that caused that youth to cleave to him like a burr all
the evening.

The young people scattered over the rocks, and hastened to visit
the points of interest before dark. They climbed the lighthouse
tower, and paid Aunt Nabby and Grandpa a call at the weather-
beaten little house, where the old woman lent them a mammoth
coffeepot, and promised that Ruth would "dish up them fish in
good shape at eight punctooal." Then they strolled away to see the
fresh-water pond where the lilies grew.

"How curious that such a thing should be here right in the middle of the salt sea!" said one of the girls, as they stood looking at the quiet pool while the tide dashed high upon the rocks all about them.

"Not more curious than how it is possible for anything so beautiful and pure as one of those lilies to grow from the mud at the bottom of the pond. The ugly yellow ones are not so out of place; but no one cares for them, and they smell horridly," added another girl in a reflective tone.

"Instinct sends the white lily straight up to the sun and air, and the strong slender stem anchors it to the rich earth below, out of which it has power to draw the nourishment that makes it so lovely and keeps it spotless — unless slugs and flies and boys spoil it," added Miss Scott as she watched Mr. Fred poke and splash with his cane after a half-closed flower.

"The naughty things have all shut up and spoilt the pretty sight; I'm so disappointed," sighed Miss Ellery, surveying the green buds with great disfavor as she had planned to wear some in her hair and act Undine.

"You must come early in the morning if you want to see them at their best. I've read somewhere that when the sun first strikes them they open rapidly, and it is a lovely sight. I shall try to see it some day if I can get here in time," said Miss Scott.

"How romantic old maids are!" whispered one girl to another.

"So are young ones; hear what Floss Ellery is saying," answered the other; and both giggled under their big hats as they caught these words followed by the rippling laugh:

"All flowers open and show their hearts when the sun shines on them at the right moment."

"I wish human flowers would," murmured Mr. Fred; and then, as if rather alarmed at his own remark, he added hastily, "I'll get that big lily out there and *make* it bloom for you."

Trusting to an old log that lay in the pond, he went to the end and bent to pull in the half-shut flower; but this too ardent sun was not to make it blossom, for his foot slipped and down he went up to his knees in mud and water.

"Save him! Oh, save him!" shrieked Miss Ellery, clutching Captain John, who was laughing like a boy, while the other lads shouted and the girls added their shrill merriment as poor Fred scrambled to the shore, a wreck of the gallant craft that had set sail in spotless white.

"What the deuce shall I do?" he asked in a tone of despair as they flocked about him to condole even while they laughed.

"Roll up your trousers and borrow Sam's boots. The old lady will dry your shoes and socks while you are at supper, and have them ready to wear home," suggested Captain John, who was used to duckings and made light of them.

The word "supper" made one carnal-minded youth sniff the air and announce that he smelt "something good"; and at once every-one turned toward the picnic ground, like chickens hurrying to the barn at feeding time. Fred vanished into the cottage, and the rest gathered about the great fire of driftwood fast turning to clear coals, over which Ruth was beginning her long hot task. She wore a big apron, a red handkerchief over her head, had her sleeves rolled up, and was so intent on her work that she merely nodded and smiled as the newcomers greeted her with varying degrees of courtesy.

"She looks like a handsome gypsy, with her dark face and that red thing in the firelight. I wish I could paint her," said Miss Scott, who was very young at heart in spite of her fifty years and gray head.

"So do I, but we can remember it. I do like to see a girl work with a will, even at frying fish. Most of 'em dawdle so at the few things they try to do. There's a piece of energy for you!" and Captain John leaned forward from his rocky seat to watch Ruth, who just then caught up the coffee pot about to boil over, and with the other hand saved her frying pan from capsizing on its unsteady bed of coals.

"She is a nice girl, and I'm much interested in her. Mr. Wallace says he will tell us her story by and by if we care to hear it. He has known the old man a long time."

"Don't forget to remind him, Aunty. I like a yarn after mess"; and Captain John went off to bring the first plate of fish to the dear old lady who had been a mother to him for many years.

It was a merry supper, and the moon was up before it ended; for everything "tasted so good" the hearty young appetites sharpened by sea air were hard to satisfy. When the last cunner had vanished and nothing but olives and oyster crackers remained, the party settled on a sloping rock out of range of the fire, and reposed for a brief period to recover from the exertions of the feast, having, like the heroes in the old story, "eaten mightily for the space of an hour."

Mr. Fred in the capacious boots was a never-failing source of amusement, and consequently somewhat subdued. But Miss Ellery consoled him, and much food sustained him till his shoes were dry. Ruth remained to clear up, and Sammy to gorge himself on the remnants of "sweet cake" which he could not bear to see wasted. So, when someone proposed telling stories till they were ready to sing, Mr. Wallace was begged to begin.

"It is only something about this island, but you may like to hear it just now," said the genial old gentleman, settling his handkerchief over his bald head for fear of cold, and glancing at the attentive young faces grouped about him in the moonlight.

"Some twenty years ago there was a wreck over there on those great rocks; you fellows have heard about it, so I'll only say that a very brave sailor, a native of the Port here, swam out with a rope and saved a dozen men and women. I'll call him Sam. Well, one of the women was an English governess, and when the lady she was with went on her way after the wreck, this pretty girl (who by the way was a good deal hurt trying to save the child she had in charge) was left behind to recover, and —"

"Marry the brave sailor of course," cried one of the girls.

"Exactly! And a very happy pair they were. She had no family who wanted her at home; her father had been a clergyman, I believe, and she was well-born, but Sam was a fine fellow and earned his living honestly, fishing off the Banks, as half the men do here. Well, they were very happy, had two children, and were saving up a bit, when poor Sam and two brothers were lost in one of the great storms which now and then make widows and orphans by the dozen. It killed the wife; but Sam's father, who kept the lighthouse here then, took the poor children and supported them for ten years. The boy was a mere baby; the girl a fine creature, brave like her father, handsome like her mother, and with a good deal of the lady about her, though everyone didn't find it out."

"Ahem!" cried the sharp girl, who began to understand the point of the story now, but would not spoil it, as the others seemed still in the dark, though Miss Scott was smiling, and Captain John staring hard at the old gentleman in the blue silk nightcap.

"Got a fly in your throat?" asked a neighbor; but Kate only laughed and begged pardon for interrupting.

"There's not much more; only that affair was rather romantic, and one can't help wondering how the children turned out. Storms seem to have been their doom, for in the terrible one we had two winters ago, the old lighthouse-keeper had a bad fall on the icy rocks, and if it had not been for the girl, the light would have gone out and more ships been lost on this dangerous point. The keeper's mate had gone ashore and couldn't get back for two days, the gale raged so fiercely; but he knew Ben could get on without him, as he had the girl and boy over for a visit. In winter they lived with a friend and went to school at the Port. It would have been all right if Ben hadn't broken his ribs. But he was a stout old salt; so he told the girl what to do, and she did it, while the boy waited on the sick man. For two days and nights that brave creature lived in the tower, that often rocked as if it would come down, while the sleet and snow dimmed the lantern, and sea birds were beaten to death against the glass. But the light burned steadily, and people said,

'All is well,' as ships steered away in time, when the clear light warned them of danger, and grateful sailors blessed the hands that kept it burning faithfully."

"I hope she got rewarded," cried an eager voice, as the story-teller paused for breath.

" 'I only did my duty; that is reward enough,' she said, when some of the rich men at the Port heard of it and sent her money and thanks. She took the money, however, for Ben had to give up the place, being too lame to do the work. He earns his living by fishing now, and puts away most of his pension for the children. He won't last long, and then they must take care of themselves; for the old woman is no relation, and the girl is too proud to hunt up the forgetful English friends, if they have any. But I don't fear for her; a brave lass like that will make her own way anywhere."

"Is that all?" asked several voices, as Mr. Wallace leaned back and fanned himself with his hat.

"That's all of the first and second parts; the third is yet to come. When I know it, I'll tell you; perhaps next summer, if we meet here again."

"Then you know the girl? What is she doing now?" asked Miss Ellery, who had lost a part of the story as she sat in a shadowy nook with the pensive Fred.

"We all know her. She is washing a coffeepot at this moment, I believe." And Mr. Wallace pointed to a figure on the beach, ener-getically shaking a large tin article that shone in the moonlight.

"Ruth? Really? How romantic and interesting!" exclaimed Miss Ellery, who was just of the age, as were most of the other girls, to enjoy tales of this sort and imagine sensational *dénoue-ments.*

"There is a great deal of untold romance in the lives of these toilers of the sea, and I am sure this good girl will find her reward for the care she takes of the old man and the boy. It costs her something, I've discovered, for she wants an education, and could get it if she left this poor place and lived for herself; but she won't go, and works hard to get money for Grandpa's comfort, instead of buying the books she longs for. I think, young ladies, that there is real heroism in cheerfully selling lilies and frying fish for duty's sake when one longs to be studying, and enjoying a little of the youth that comes but once," said Mr. Wallace.

"Oh dear, yes, so nice of her! We might take up a contribution for her when we get home. I'll head the paper with pleasure and give all I can afford, for it must be so horrid to be ignorant at her age. I dare say the poor thing can't even read; just fancy!" and Miss Ellery clasped her hands with a sigh of pity.

"Very few girls can read fit to be heard nowadays," murmured Miss Scott.

"Don't let them affront her with their money; she will fling it in their faces as she did that donkey's dollar. You see to her in your nice, delicate way, Aunty, and give her a lift if she will let you," whispered Captain John in the old lady's ear.

"Don't waste your pity, Miss Florence. Ruth reads a newspaper better than any woman I ever knew. I've heard her doing it to the old man, getting through shipping news, money-market, and politics in fine style. I wouldn't offer her money if I were you, though it is a kind thought. These people have an honest pride in earning things for themselves, and I respect them for it," added Mr. Wallace.

"Dear me! I should as soon think of a sand-skipper having pride as one of these fishy folks in this stupid little place," observed Mr. Fred, moving his legs into the shadow as the creeping moonlight began to reveal the hideous boots.

"Why not? I think they have more to be proud of, these brave, honest, independent people, than many who never earn a cent and swell around on the money their fathers made out of pork, rum, or — any other rather unpleasant or disreputable business," said Captain John, with the twinkle in his eye, as he changed the end of his sentence, for the word "pickles" was on his lips when Aunt Mary's quick touch checked it. Some saucy girl laughed, and Mr.

Fred squirmed, for it was well known that his respectable grand-father whom he never mentioned had made his large fortune in a pickle-factory.

"We all rise from the mud in one sense, and all may be hand-some flowers if we choose before we go back, after blooming, to ripen our seeds at the bottom of the water where we began," said Miss Scott's refined voice, sounding softly after the masculine ones.

"I like that idea! Thank you, Aunt Mary, for giving me such a pretty fancy to add to my love for water lilies. I shall remember it, and try to be a lovely one, not a bit ashamed to own that I came from honest farmer stock," exclaimed the thoughtful girl who had learned to know and love the sweet, wise woman who was so motherly to all girls.

"Hear! hear!" cried Captain John, heartily; for he was very proud of his own brave name kept clean and bright through a long line of sailor kin.

"Now let us sing or we shall have no time," suggested Miss Ellery, who warbled as well as rippled, and did not wish to lose this opportunity of singing certain sentimental songs appropriate to the hour.

So they tuned their pipes and made "music in the air" for an hour, to the great delight of Sammy, who joined in every song, and was easily persuaded to give sundry nautical melodies in a shrill small voice which convulsed his hearers with merriment.

"Ruth sings awful well, but she won't afore folks," he said, as he paused after a roaring ditty.

"She will for me," and Mr. Wallace went slowly up to the rock not far away, where Ruth sat alone listening to the music as she rested after her long day's work.

"Such airs!" said Miss Ellery, in a sharp tone; for her "Wind of the Summer Night" had not gone well, owing to a too copious supper. "Posing for Lorelei," she added, as Ruth began to sing, glad to oblige the kind old gentleman. They expected some queer ballad or droning hymn, and were surprised when a clear sweet voice gave them "The Three Fishers" and "Mary on the Sands of Dee" with a simple pathos that made real music lovers thrill with pleasure, and filled several pairs of eyes with tears.

"More, please, more!" called Captain John, as she paused; and as if encouraged by the hearty applause her one gift excited, she sang on as easily as a bird till her small store was exhausted.

"I call *that* music," said Miss Scott, as she wiped her eyes with a sigh of satisfaction. "It comes from the heart and goes to the heart, as it should. Now we don't want anything else, and had better go home while the spell lasts."

Most of the party followed her example, and went to thank and say good-night to Ruth, who felt as rich and happy as a queen with the money Mr. Wallace had slipped into her pocket, and the pleasure which even this short glimpse of a higher, happier life had brought her hungry nature.

As the boats floated away, leaving her alone on the shore, she sent her farewell ringing over the water in the words of the old song, "A Life on the Ocean Wave"; and everyone joined in it with a will, especially Mr. Wallace and Captain John; and so the evening picnic ended tunefully and pleasantly for all, and was long remembered by several.

After that day, many "good times" came to Ruth and Sammy; and even poor old Grandpa had his share, finding the last summer of his life very smooth sailing as he slowly drifted into port. It seemed quite natural that Captain John, being a sailor, should like to go and read and "yarn" with the old fisherman; so no one wondered when he fell into the way of rowing over to the Island very often with his pocket full of newspapers, and whiling away the long hours in the little house as full of sea smells and salt breezes as a shell on the shore.

Miss Scott also took a fancy to go with her nephew; for, being an ardent botanist, she discovered that the Island possessed many plants which she could not find on the rocky point of land where

the hotel and cottages stood. The fresh-water pond was her especial delight, and it became a sort of joke to ask, when she came
home brown and beaming with her treasures in tin boxes, bottles,
and bunches:

"Well, Aunt Mary, have you seen the water lilies bloom yet?"
and she always answered with that wise smile of hers:

"Not yet, but I'm biding my time, and am watching a very fine
one with especial interest. When the right moment comes, it will
bloom and show its golden heart to me, I hope."

Ruth never quite knew how it came about, but books seemed to
find their way to the Island and stay there, to her great delight. A
demand for lilies sprang up, and when their day was over marsh-
rosemary became the rage. Sammy found a market for all the
shells and gulls' wings he could furnish, and certain old curiosities
brought from many voyages were sold for sums which added
many comforts to the old sailor's last cruise.

Now the daily row to the Point was a pleasure, not a trial, to
Ruth — for Mr. Wallace was always ready with a kind word or
gift; the ladies nodded as she passed, and asked how the old Skipper was today; Miss Scott often told her to stop at the cottage for
some new book or a moment's chat on her way to the boat, and
Captain John helped Sammy with his fishing so much that the
baskets were always full when they came home.

All this help and friendliness put a wonderful energy and sweetness into Ruth's hard life, and made her work seem light, her patient waiting for freedom easier to bear cheerfully. She sang as she
stood over her washtub, cheered the long nights of watching with
the precious books, and found the few moments of rest that came
to her when the day's work was done very pleasant, as she sat on
her rock, watching the lights from the Point, catching the sound
of gay music as the young people danced, and thinking over the
delightful talks she had with Miss Scott. Perhaps the presence of a
blue jacket in Grandpa's little bedroom, the sight of a friendly
brown face smiling when she came in, and the sonorous murmur

of a man's voice reading aloud, added a charm to the girl's hum-drum life. She was too innocent and frank to deny that she enjoyed these new friends, and welcomed both with the same eagerness, saw both go with the same regret, and often wondered how she ever had got on without them.

But the modest fisher-maiden never dreamed of any warmer feeling than kindness on the one side and gratitude on the other; and this unconsciousness was her greatest charm, especially to Captain John, who hated coquettes, and shunned the silly girls who wasted time in idle flirtation when they had far better and wholesomer pastimes to enjoy. The handsome sailor was a favorite, being handy at all sorts of fun, and the oldest of the young men at the Point. He was very courteous in his hearty way to every woman he met, from the stateliest dowager to the dowdiest waiter-girl, but devoted himself entirely to Aunt Mary, and seemed to have no eyes for younger fairer faces.

"He must have a sweetheart over the sea somewhere," the dam-sels said among themselves, as they watched him pace the long piazzas alone, or saw him swinging in his hammock with eyes dreamily fixed on the blue bay before him.

Miss Scott only smiled when curious questions were asked her, and said she hoped John would find his mate sometime, for he deserved the best wife in the world, having been a good son and an honest boy for six-and-twenty years.

"What is it, Captain — a steamer?" asked Mr. Fred, as he came by the cottage one August afternoon, with his usual escort of girls, all talking at once about some very interesting affair.

"Only a sailboat; no steamers today," answered Captain John, dropping the glass from his eye with a start.

"Can you see people on the Island with that thing? We want to know if Ruth is at home, because if she isn't we can't waste time going over," said Miss Ellery, with her sweetest smile.

"I think not. That boat is Sammy's, and as there is a speck of red aboard, I fancy Miss Ruth is with him. They are coming this way, so you can hail them if you like," answered the sailor, with "a speck of red" on his own sunburnt cheek if any one cared to look.

"Then we'll wait here if we may. We ordered her to bring us a quantity of bulrushes and flowers for our tableaux tonight, and we want her to be Rebecca at the well. She is so dark, and with her hair down, and gold bangles and scarlet shawls, I think she would do nicely. It takes so long to arrange the 'Lily Maid of Astolat' we *must* have an easy one to come just before that, and the boys are wild to make a camel of themselves, so we planned this. Won't you be Jacob or Abraham or whoever the man with the bracelets was?" asked Miss Ellery, as they all settled on the steps in the free-and-easy way which prevailed at the Point.

"No, thank you, I don't act. Used to dance hornpipes in my young days, but gave up that sort of thing some time ago."

"How unfortunate! Everyone acts; it's all the fashion," began Miss Ellery, rolling up her blue eyes imploringly.

"So I see; but I never cared much for theatricals, I like natural things better."

"How unkind you are! I quite depended on you for that, since you wouldn't be a corsair."

"Fred's the man for such fun. He's going to startle the crowd with a regular Captain Kidd rig, pistols and cutlasses enough for a whole crew, and a terrific beard."

"I know Ruth won't do it, Floss, for she looked amazed when I showed her my Undine costume, and told her what I wanted the seaweed for. 'Why, you won't stand before all those folks dressed that way, will you?' she said, as much scandalized as if she'd never seen a low-necked dress and silk stockings before"; and Miss Perry tossed her head with an air of pity for a girl who could be surprised at the display of a pretty neck and arms and ankles.

"We'll *hire* her, then; she's a mercenary wretch and will do anything for money. I won't be scrambled into my boat in a hurry, and we *must* have Rebecca because I've borrowed a fine pitcher and promised the boys their camel," said Miss Ellery, who considered herself the queen of the place and ruled like one, in virtue of being the prettiest girl there and the richest.

"She has landed, I think, for the boat is off again to the wharf. Better run down and help her with the bulrushes, Fred, and the rest of the stuff you ordered," suggested Captain John, longing to go himself but kept by his duty as host, Aunt Mary being asleep upstairs.

"Too tired. Won't hurt her; she's used to work, and we mustn't pamper her up, as old ladies say," answered Mr. Fred, enjoying his favorite lounge on the grass.

"I wouldn't ask her to act, if you'll allow me to say so," said Captain John, in his quiet way. "That sort of thing might unsettle her and make her discontented. She steers that little craft over there and is happy now; let her shape her own course, and remember it isn't well to talk to the man at the wheel."

Miss Perry stared; Miss Ray, the sharp girl, nodded, and Miss Ellery said petulantly:

"As if it mattered what *she* thought or said or did! It's her place to be useful if we want her, and we needn't worry about spoiling a girl like that. She can't be any prouder or more saucy than she is, and I shall ask her if only to see the airs she will put on."

As she spoke Ruth came up the sandy path from the beach laden with rushes and weeds, sunflowers and shells, looking warm and tired but more picturesque than ever, in her blue gown and the red handkerchief she wore since her old hat blew away. Seeing the party on the cottage steps, she stopped to ask if the things were right, and Miss Ellery at once made her request in a commanding tone which caused Ruth to grow very straight and cool and sober all at once, and answer decidedly:

"I couldn't anyway."

"Why not?"

"Well, one reason is I don't think it's right to act things out of the Bible just to show off and amuse folks."

"The idea of minding!" and Miss Ellery frowned, adding angrily, "We will pay you for it. I find people will do anything for money down here."

"We are poor and need it, and this is our best time to make it. I'd do most anything to earn a little, but not that," and Ruth looked as proud as the young lady herself.

"Then we'll say no more if you are too elegant to do what *we* don't mind at all. I'll pay you for this stuff now, as I ordered it, and you needn't bring me any more. How much do I owe you?" asked the offended beauty, taking out her purse in a pet.

"Nothing. I'm glad to oblige the ladies if I can, for they have been very kind to me. Perhaps if you knew why I want to earn money, you'd understand me better. Grandpa can't last long, and I don't want the town to bury him. I'm working and saving so he can be buried decently, as he wants to be, not like a pauper."

There was something in Ruth's face and voice as she said this, standing there shabby, tired, and heavy-laden, yet honest, dutiful and patient for love's sake, that touched the hearts of those who looked and listened; but she left no time for any answer, for with the last word she went on quickly, as if to hide the tears that dimmed her clear eyes and the quiver of her lips.

"Floss, how could you!" cried Miss Ray, and ran to take the sheaf of bulrushes from Ruth's arms, followed by the rest, all ashamed and repentant now that a word had shown them the hard life going on beside their idle, carefree ones.

Captain John longed to follow, but walked into the house, growling to himself with a grim look:

"That girl has no more heart than a butterfly, and I'd like to see her squirm on a pin! Poor Ruth! We'll settle that matter, and bury old Ben like an admiral, hang me if we don't!"

He was so busy talking the affair over with Aunt Mary that he did not see the girl flit by to wait for her boat on the beach, having steadily refused the money offered her, though she accepted the apologies in the kindest spirit.

The beach at this hour of the day was left to the nurses and

maids who bathed and gossiped while the little people played in
the sand or paddled in the sea. Several were splashing about, and
one German governess was scolding violently because while she
was in the bathhouse her charge, a little girl of six, had rashly
ventured out in a flat-bottomed tub, as they called the small boats
used by the gentlemen to reach the yachts anchored in deep water.

Ruth saw the child's danger at a glance, for the tide was going
out, carrying the frail cockleshell rapidly away, while the child
risked an upset every moment by stretching her arms to the women
on the shore and calling them to help her.

None dared to try, but all stood and wrung their hands, screaming like seagulls, till the girl, throwing off shoes and heavy skirt,
plunged in, calling cheerily, "Sit still! I'll come and get you,
Milly!"

She could swim like a fish, but encumbered with her clothes and
weary with an unusually hard day's work, she soon found that she
did not gain as rapidly as she expected upon the receding boat.
She did not lose courage, but a thrill of anxiety shot through her
as she felt her breath grow short, her limbs heavy, and the tide
sweep her farther and farther from the shore.

"If they would only stop screaming and go for help, I could
keep up and push the boat in; but the child will be out presently
and then we are lost, for I can't get back with her, I'm afraid."

As these thoughts passed through her mind Ruth was swim-
ming stoutly, and trying by cheerful words to keep the frightened
child from risking their main chance of safety. A few more strokes
and she would reach the boat, rest a moment, then, clinging to it,
push it leisurely to shore. Feeling that the danger was over, she
hurried on and was just putting up her hands to seize the frail raft
and get her breath when Milly, thinking she was to be taken in her
arms, leaned forward. In rushed the water, down went the boat,
and out splashed the screaming child to cling to Ruth with the
desperate clutch she dreaded.

Both went under for a moment, but rose again; and with all her wits sharpened by the peril of the moment, Ruth cried, as she kept herself afloat:

"On my back, quick! quick! Don't touch my arms; hold tight to my hair, and keep still."

Not realizing all the danger, and full of faith in Ruth's power to do anything, after the feats of diving and floating she had seen her perform, Milly scrambled up as often before, and clung spluttering and grasping to Ruth's strong shoulders. So burdened, and conscious of fast-failing strength, Ruth turned toward the shore, and bent every power of mind and body to her task. How far away it seemed! How still the women were — not one even venturing out a little way to help her, and no man in sight! Her heart seemed to stop beating, her temples throbbed, her breath was checked by the clinging arms, and the child seemed to grow heavier every moment.

"I'll do what I can, but, oh, why don't someone come?"

That was the last thought Ruth was conscious of, as she panted and ploughed slowly back, with such a set white face and wide eyes fixed on the flag that fluttered from the nearest cottage, that it was no wonder the women grew still as they watched her. One good Catholic nurse fell on her knees to pray; the maids cried, the governess murmured, "Mein Gott, I am lost if the child go drowned!" and clear and sweet came the sound of Captain John's whistle as he stood on his piazza waiting to row Ruth home.

They were nearly in, a few more strokes and she could touch the bottom, when suddenly all grew black before her eyes, and whispering, "I'll float. Call, Milly, and don't mind me," Ruth turned over, still holding the child fast, and with nothing but her face out of water, feebly struggled on.

"Come and get me! She's going down! Oh, come, quick!" called the child in a tone of such distress that the selfish German bestirred herself at last, and began to wade cautiously in. Seeing help at hand, brave little Milly soon let go, and struck out like an energetic young frog, while Ruth, quite spent, sank quietly down, with a dim sense that her last duty was done and rest had come.

The shrill cries of the women when they saw the steady white face disappear and rise no more, reached Captain John's ear, and sent him flying down the path, sure that someone was in danger.

"Ruth — gone down — out there!" was all he caught, as many voices tried to tell the tale; and waiting for no more, he threw off hat and coat, and dashed into the sea as if ready to search the Atlantic till he found her.

She was safe in a moment, and pausing only to send one girl flying for the doctor, he carried his streaming burden straight home to Aunt Mary, who had her between blankets before a soul arrived, and was rubbing for dear life while John fired up the spirit lamp for hot brandy and water, with hands that trembled as he splashed about like an agitated Newfoundland fresh from a swim.

Ruth was soon conscious, but too much exhausted to do or say anything, and lay quietly suffering the discomforts of resuscitation till she fell asleep.

"Is Milly safe?" was all she asked, and being assured that the child was in her mother's arms, and Sammy had gone to tell Grandpa all about it, she smiled and shut her eyes with a whispered, "Then it's all right, thank God!"

All that evening Captain John paced the piazza, and warned away the eager callers, who flocked down to ask about the heroine of the hour; for she was more interesting then Undine, the Lily Maid, or any of the pretty creatures attitudinizing behind the red curtains in the hot hotel parlor. All that night Aunt Mary watched the deep sleep that restored the girl, and now and then crept out to tell her nephew there was nothing to fear for one so strong and healthful. And all night Ruth dreamed strange dreams, some weird and dim, some full of pain and fear; but as the fever of reaction passed away, lovely visions of a happy place came to her,

where faces she loved were near, and rest, and all she longed for
was hers at last. So clear and beautiful was this dream that she
waked in the early dawn to lie and think of it, with such a look of
peace upon her face that Aunt Mary could not but kiss it tenderly
when she came in to see if all was well.

"How are you, dear? Has this nice long sleep set you up again
as I hoped?"

"Oh yes, I'm quite well, thank you, and I must go home.
Grandpa will worry so till he sees me," answered Ruth, sitting up
with her wet hair on her shoulders, and a little shiver of pain as she
stretched her tired arms.

"Not yet, my dear; rest another hour or two and have some
breakfast. Then, if you like, John shall take you home before anyone comes to plague you with idle questions. I'm not going to say a
word, except that I'm proud of my brave girl, and mean to take
care of her if she will let me."

With that and a motherly embrace, the old lady bustled away to
stir up her maid and wake John from his first nap with the smell
of coffee, a most unromantic but satisfying perfume to all the
weary watchers in the house.

An hour later, dressed in Miss Scott's gray wrapper and rose-
colored shawl, Ruth came slowly to the beach leaning on Captain
John's arm, while Aunt Mary waved her napkin from the rocks
above, and sent kind messages after them as they pushed off.

It was the loveliest hour of all the day. The sun had not yet risen,
but sea and sky were rosy with the flush of dawn; the small waves
rippled up the sand, the wind blew fresh and fragrant from hayfields far away, and in the grove the birds were singing, as they
only sing at peep of day. A still, soft, happy time before the work
and worry of the world began, the peaceful moment which is so
precious to those who have learned to love its balm and consecrate
its beauty with their prayers.

Ruth sat silent, looking about her as if she saw anew heaven
and earth, and had no words in which to tell the feeling that

made her eyes so soft, sent the fresh color back into her cheeks, and touched her lips with something sweeter than a smile.

Captain John rowed very slowly, watching her with a new expression in his face; and when she drew a long breath, a happy sort of sigh, he leaned forward to ask, as if he knew what brought it:

"You are glad to be alive, Ruth?"

"Oh, so glad! I didn't want to die; life's very pleasant now," she answered, with her frank eyes meeting his so gratefully.

"Even though it's hard?"

"It's easier lately; you and dear Miss Mary have helped so much, I see my way clear, and mean to go right on, real brave and cheerful, sure I'll get my wish at last."

"So do I!" and Captain John laughed a queer, happy laugh, as he bent to his oars again, with the look of a man who knew where he was going and longed to get there as soon as possible.

"I hope you will. I wish I could help anyway to pay for all you've done for me. I know you don't want to be thanked for fishing me up, but I mean to do it all the same, if I can, sometime"; and Ruth's voice was full of tender energy as she looked down into the deep green water where her life would have ended but for him.

"What did you think of when you went down so quietly? Those women said you never called for help once."

"I had no breath to call. I knew you were near, I hoped you'd come, and I thought of poor Grandpa and Sammy as I gave up and seemed to go to sleep."

A very simple answer, but it made Captain John beam with delight; and the morning red seemed to glow all over his brown face as he rowed across the quiet bay, looking at Ruth sitting opposite, so changed by the soft becoming colors of her dress, the late danger, and the dreams that still lingered in her mind, making it hard to feel that she was the same girl who went that way only a day ago.

Presently the Captain spoke again in a tone that was both eager and anxious:

"I'm glad my idle summer hasn't been quite wasted. It's over now, and I'm off in a few days for a year's cruise, you know."

"Yes, Miss Mary told me you were going soon. I'll miss you both, but maybe you'll come next year?"

"I will, please God!"

"So will I; for even if I get away this fall, I'd love to come again in summer and rest a little while, no matter what I find to do."

"Come and stay with Aunt Mary if this home is gone. I shall want Sammy next time. I've settled that with the Skipper, you know, and I'll take good care of the little chap. He's not much younger than I was when I shipped for my first voyage. You'll let him go?"

"Anywhere with you. He's set his heart on being a sailor, and Grandpa likes it. All our men are, and I'd be one if I were a boy. I love the sea so, I couldn't be happy long away from it."

"Even though it nearly drowned you?"

"Yes, I'd rather die that way than any other. But it was my fault; I shouldn't have failed if I hadn't been so tired. I've often swum farther; but I'd been three hours in the marsh getting those things for the girls, and it was washing-day, and I'd been up nearly all night with Grandpa; so don't blame the sea, please, Captain John."

"You should have called me; I was waiting for you, Ruth."

"I didn't know it. I'm used to doing things myself. It might have been too late for Milly if I'd waited."

"Thank God, I wasn't too late for you."

The boat was at the shore now; and as he spoke Captain John held out his hands to help Ruth down, for, encumbered with her long dress, and still weak from past suffering, she could not spring to land as she used to do in her short gown. For the first time the color deepened in her cheek as she looked into the face before her and read the meaning of the eyes that found her beautiful and dear, and the lips that thanked God for her salvation so fervently.

She did not speak, but let him lift her down, draw her hand through his arm, and lead her up the rocky slope to the little pool that lay waiting for the sun's first rays to wake from its sleep. He paused there, and with his hand on hers said quietly:

"Ruth, before I go I want to tell you something, and this is a good time and place. While Aunt Mary watched the flowers, I've watched you, and found the girl I've always wanted for my wife. Modest and brave, dutiful and true, that's what I love; could you give me all this, dear, for the little I can offer, and next year sail with Sammy and a very happy man if you say yes?"

"I'm not half good and wise enough for that! Remember what I am," began Ruth, bending her head as if the thought were more than she could bear.

"I do remember, and I'm proud of it! Why, dear heart, I've worked my way up from a common sailor, and am the better for it. Now I've got my ship, and I want a mate to make a home for me aboard and ashore. Look up and tell me that I didn't read those true eyes wrong."

Then Ruth lifted up her face, and the sunshine showed him all he asked to know, as she answered with her heart in her voice and the "true eyes" fixed on his:

"I tried not to love you, knowing what a poor ignorant girl I am; but you were so kind to me, how could I help it, John?"

That satisfied him, and he sealed his happy thanks on the innocent lips none had kissed but the little brother, the old man, and the fresh winds of the sea.

One can imagine the welcome they met at the small brown house, and what went on inside as Grandpa blessed the lovers, and Sammy so overflowed with joy at his enchanting prospects, that he was obliged to vent his feelings in ecstatic jigs upon the beach, to the great amazement of the gulls and sandpipers at breakfast there.

No one at the Point, except a certain dear old lady, knew the pleasant secret, though many curious or friendly visitors went to the Island that day to see the heroine and express their wonder, thanks, and admiration. All agreed that partial drowning seemed to suit the girl, for a new Ruth had risen like Venus from the sea. A softer beauty was in her fresh face now, a gentler sort of pride possessed her, and a still more modest shrinking from praise and publicity became her well. No one guessed the cause, and she was soon forgotten; for the season was over, the summer guests departed, and the Point was left to the few cottagers who loved to linger into golden September.

Miss Mary was one of these, and Captain John another; for he remained as long as he dared, to make things comfortable for the old man, and to sit among the rocks with Ruth when her day's work was done, listening while his "Mermaid," as he called her, sang as she had never sung before, and let him read the heart he had made his own, for the lily was wide open now, and its gold all his.

With the first frosts Grandpa died, and was carried to his grave by his old comrades, owing no man a cent, thanks to his dutiful granddaughter and the new son she had given him. Then the little house was deserted, and all winter Ruth was happy with Aunt Mary, while Sammy studied bravely, and lived on dreams of the joys in store for him when the Captain came sailing home again.

Another summer brought the happy day when the little brown house was set in order for a sailor's honeymoon, when the flag floated gaily over Miss Mary's cottage, and Ruth in a white gown with her chosen flowers in her hair and bosom, shipped with her dear Captain for the long cruise which had its storms and calms, but never any shipwreck of the love that grew and blossomed with the water lilies by the sea.

LAURIE

from *Aunt Jo's Scrap Bag*
(Volume I), 1871

That first journey to Europe, already spoken of as one of the important experiences of Louisa's life, was made more memorable by her acquaintance and later warm friendship with the boy whom she called Laurie and put, second only to Jo, among the characters in Little Women. *The overflowing admiration of the real Laurie, the Polish boy Ladislas, was a heart-warming surprise to Louisa and did her much good since her own opinion of herself was very small. In his place in* Little Women, *he is one of her best-drawn and appealing figures. She has captured very fully what must have been his real charm, his integrity, his courtesy, his courageous and affectionate nature. It is of interest, in this account of him, which is part of a longer reminiscent sketch of the boys she has known, to see what were the aspects of the original of Laurie.*

LAURIE

Feeling that I have been unusually fortunate in my knowledge of a choice and pleasing variety of this least appreciated portion of the human race, I have a fancy to record some of my experiences, hoping that it may awaken an interest in other minds, and cause other people to cultivate the delightful, but too often neglected boys, who now run to waste, so to speak. . . .

The best and dearest of all my flock was my Polish boy, Ladislas Wisniewski — two hiccoughs and a sneeze will give you the name perfectly. Six years ago, as I went down to my early breakfast at our Pension in Vevey, I saw that a stranger had arrived. He was a tall youth of eighteen or twenty, with a thin, intelligent face, and the charmingly polite manners of a foreigner. As the other boarders came in, one by one, they left the door open, and a draught of cold autumn air blew in from the stone corridor, making the newcomer cough, shiver, and cast wistful glances toward the warm corner by the stove. My place was there, and the heat often oppressed me, so I was glad of an opportunity to move.

A word to Madame Vodoz effected the change; and at dinner I was rewarded by a grateful smile from the poor fellow, as he nestled into his warm seat, after a pause of surprise and a flush of pleasure at the small kindness from a stranger. We were too far apart to talk much, but, as he filled his glass, the Pole bowed to me, and said low in French:

"I drink the good health to Mademoiselle."

I returned the wish, but he shook his head with a sudden

shadow on his face, as if the words meant more than mere compliment to him.

"That boy is sick and needs care. I must see to him," said I to
myself, as I met him in the afternoon, and observed the military
look of his blue and white suit, as he touched his cap and smiled
pleasantly. I have a weakness for brave boys in blue, and having
discovered that he had been in the late Polish Revolution, my heart
warmed to him at once.

That evening he came to me in the salon, and expressed his
thanks in the prettiest broken English I ever heard. So simple,
frank, and grateful was he that a few words of interest won his
little story from him, and in half an hour we were friends. With
his fellow-students he had fought through the last outbreak, had
suffered imprisonment and hardship rather than submit, had lost
many friends, his fortune and his health, and at twenty, lonely,
poor, and ill, was trying bravely to cure the malady which seemed
fatal.

"If I recover myself of this affair in the chest, I teach the music
to acquire my bread in this so hospitable country. At Paris, my
friends, all two, find a refuge, and I go to them in spring if I die
not here. Yes, it is solitary, and my memories are not gay, but I
have my work, and the good God remains always to me, so I content myself with much hope, and I wait."

Such genuine piety and courage increased my respect and regard immensely, and a few minutes later he added to both by one
of the little acts that show character better than words.

He told me about the massacre, when five hundred Poles were
shot down by Cossacks in the market-place, merely because they
sang their national hymn.

"Play me that forbidden air," I said, wishing to judge of his
skill, for I had heard him practicing softly in the afternoon.

He rose willingly, then glanced about the room and gave a little
shrug which made me ask what he wanted.

"I look to see if the Baron is here. He is Russian, and to him my national air will not be pleasing."

"Then play it. He dare not forbid it here, and I should rather enjoy that little insult to your bitter enemy," said I, feeling very indignant with everything Russian just then.

"Ah, mademoiselle, it is true we are enemies, but we are also gentlemen," returned the boy, proving that *he* at least was one.

I thanked him for his lesson in politeness, and as the Baron was not there he played the beautiful hymn, singing it enthusiastically in spite of the danger to his weak lungs. A true musician evidently, for as he sang his pale face glowed, his eyes shone, and his lost vigor seemed restored to him.

From that evening we were fast friends; for the memory of certain dear lads at home made my heart open to this lonely boy, who gave me in return the most grateful affection and service. He begged me to call him "Varjo," as his mother did. He constituted himself my escort, errand-boy, French teacher, and private musician, making those weeks infinitely pleasant by his winning ways, his charming little confidences, and faithful friendship.

We had much fun over our lessons, for I helped him about his English. With a great interest in free America, and an intense longing to hear about our war, the barrier of an unknown tongue did not long stand between us. Beginning with my bad French and his broken English, we got on capitally; but he outdid me entirely, making astonishing progress, though he often slapped his forehead with the despairing exclamation:

"I am imbecile! I never can will shall to have learn this beast of English!"

But he did, and in a month had added a new language to the five he already possessed.

His music was the delight of the house; and he often gave us little concerts with the help of Madam Teiblin, a German St. Cecelia, with a cropped head and a gentlemanly sack, cravat, and collar. Both were enthusiasts, and the longer they played the more inspired they got. The piano vibrated, the stools creaked, the candles danced in their sockets, and everyone sat mute while the four white hands chased one another up and down the keys, and the two fine faces beamed with such ecstacy that we almost expected to see instrument and performers disappear in a musical whirlwind.

Lake Leman will never seem so lovely again as when Laddie and I roamed about its shores, floated on its bosom, or laid splendid plans for the future in the sunny garden of the old château. I tried it again last year, but the charm was gone, for I missed my boy with his fun, his music, and the frank, fresh affection he gave his "little mamma," as he insisted on calling the lofty spinster who loved him like half a dozen grandmothrs rolled into one.

December roses blossomed in the gardens then, and Laddie never failed to have a posy ready for me at dinner. Few evenings passed without "confidences" in my corner of the salon, and I still have a pile of merry little notes which I used to find tucked under my door. He called them chapters of a great history we were to write together, and being a *polisson* he illustrated it with droll pictures, and a funny mixture of French and English romance.

It was very pleasant, but like all pleasant things in this world of change it soon came to an end. When I left for Italy we jokingly agreed to meet in Paris the next May, but neither really felt that we should ever meet again, for Laddie hardly expected to outlive the winter, and I felt sure I should soon be forgotten. As he kissed my hand there were tears in my boy's eyes, and a choke in the voice that tried to say cheerfully:

"*Bon voyage*, dear and good little mamma. I do not say *adieu*, but *au revoir*."

Then the carriage rolled away, the wistful face vanished, and nothing remained to me but the memory of Laddie, and a little stain on my glove where a drop had fallen.

As I drew near Paris six months later, and found myself wish-

ing that I might meet Varjo in the great, gay city, and wondering
if there was any chance of my doing it, I never dreamed of seeing
him so soon; but, as I made my way among the crowd of passen-
gers that poured through the station, feeling tired, bewildered,
and homesick, I suddenly saw a blue and white cap wave wildly in
the air, then Laddie's beaming face appeared, and Laddie's eager
hands grasped mine so cordially that I began to laugh at once, and
felt that Paris was almost as good as home.

"Ah, ha! behold the little mamma, who did not thought to see
again her bad son! Yes, I am greatly glad that I make the fine
surprise for you as you come all weary to this place of noise. Give
to me the *billets*, for I am still mademoiselle's servant and go to
find the coffers."

He got my trunks, put me into a carriage, and as we rolled merrily away I asked how he chanced to meet me so unexpectedly.
Knowing where I intended to stay, he had called occasionally till I
notified Madame D. of the day and hour of my arrival and then he
had come to "make the fine surprise." He enjoyed the joke like a
true boy, and I was glad to see how well he looked, and how gay
he seemed.

"You are better?" I said.

"I truly hope so. The winter was good to me and I cough less. It
is a small hope, but I do not enlarge my fear by a sad face. I yet
work and save a little purse, so that I may not be a heaviness to
those who have the charity to finish me if I fall back and yet die."

I would not hear of that, and told him he looked as well and
happy as if he had found a fortune.

He laughed, and answered with his fine bow, "I have. Behold,
you come to make the *fête* for me. I find also here my friends Joseph and Napoleon. Poor as mouses of the church, as you say, but
brave boys, and we work together with much gaiety."

When I asked if he had leisure to be my guide about Paris, for
my time was short and I wanted to see *everything*, he pranced, and
told me he had promised himself a holiday, and had planned many

excursions the most wonderful, charming and gay. Then, having settled me at Madame's, he went blithely away to what I afterward discovered were very poor lodgings, across the river.

Next day began the pleasantest fortnight in all my year of travel. Laddie appeared early, elegant to behold in a new hat and buff golves, and was immensely amused because the servant informed me that my big son had arrived.

I believe the first thing a woman does in Paris is to buy a new bonnet. I did, or rather stood by and let "my son" do it in the best of French, only whispering when he proposed gorgeous *chapeaux* full of flowers and feathers, that I could not afford it.

"Ah! we must make our economies, must we? See, then, this modest, pearl-colored one, with the crepe rose. Yes, we will have that, and be most elegant for the Sunday promenade."

I fear I should have bought a pea-green hat with a yellow plume if he had urged it, so wheedlesome and droll were his ways and words. His good taste saved me, however, and the modest one was sent home for the morrow, when we were to meet Joseph and Napoleon and go to the concert in the Tuileries garden.

Then we set off on our day of sightseeing, and Laddie proved himself an excellent guide. We had a charming trip about the enchanted city, a gay lunch at a café, and a first brief glimpse of the Louvre. At dinnertime I found a posy at my place; and afterward Laddie came and spent the evening in my little salon, playing to me, and having what he called "babblings and pleasantries." I found that he was translating *Vanity Fair* into Polish, and intended to sell it at home. He convulsed me with his struggles to put cockney English and slang into good Polish, for he had saved up a list of words for me to explain to him. Haystack and bean-pot were among them, I remember; and when he had mastered the meanings he fell upon the sofa exhausted.

Other days like this followed, and we led a happy life together; for my twelve years' seniority made our adventures quite proper, and I fearlessly went anywhere on the arm of my big son. Not to theatres or balls, however, for heated rooms were bad for Laddie, but pleasant trips out of the city in the bright spring weather, quiet strolls in the gardens, moonlight concerts in the Champs-Elysées; or, best of all, long talks with music in the little red salon, with the gas turned low, and the ever-changing scenes of the Rue de Rivoli under the balcony.

Never were pleasures more cheaply purchased or more thoroughly enjoyed, for our hearts were as light as our purses, and our "little economies" gave zest to our amusements.

Joseph and Napoleon sometimes joined us, and I felt in my element with the three invalid soldier boys, for Napoleon still limped with a wound received in the war, Joseph had never recovered from his two years' imprisonment in an Austrian dungeon, and Laddie's loyalty might yet cost him his life.

Thanks to them, I discovered a joke played upon me by my *polisson*. He told me to call him *ma drogha*, saying it meant "my friend," in Polish. I innocently did so, and he seemed to find great pleasure in it, for his eyes always laughed when I said it. Using it one day before the other lads, I saw a queer twinkle in their eyes, and, suspecting mischief, demanded the real meaning of the words. Laddie tried to silence them, but the joke was too good to keep, and I found to my dismay that I had been calling him "my darling" in the tenderest manner.

How the three rascals shouted, and what a vain struggle it was to try and preserve my dignity when Laddie clasped his hands and begged pardon, explaining that jokes were necessary to his health, and he never meant me to know the full baseness of this "pleasantry!" I revenged myself by giving him some bad English for his translation, and telling him of it just as I left Paris.

It was not all fun with my boy, however; he had his troubles, and in spite of his cheerfulness he knew what heartache was. Walking in the quaint garden of the Luxembourg one day, he confided to me the little romance of his life. A very touching little romance as he told it, with eloquent eyes and voice and frequent pauses for breath. I cannot give his words, but the simple facts were these:

He had grown up with a pretty cousin, and at eighteen was desperately in love with her. She returned his affection, but they could not be happy, for her father wished her to marry a richer man. In Poland, to marry without the consent of parents is to incur lasting disgrace; so Leonore obeyed, and the young pair parted. This had been a heavy sorrow to Laddie, and he rushed into the war hoping to end his trouble.

"Do you ever hear from your cousin?" I asked, as he walked beside me, looking sadly down the green aisles where kings and queens had loved and parted years ago.

"I only know that she suffers still, for she remembers. Her husband submits to the Russians, and I despise him as I have no English to tell," and he clenched his hands with the flash of the eye and sudden kindling of the whole face that made him handsome.

He showed me a faded little picture, and when I tried to comfort him, he laid his head down on the pedestal of one of the marble queens who guard the walk, as if he never cared to lift it up again.

But he was all right in a minute, and bravely put away his sorrow with the little picture. He never spoke of it again, and I saw no more shadows on his face till we came to say good-by.

"You have been so kind to me, I wish I had something beautiful to give you, Laddie," I said, feeling that it would be hard to get on without my boy.

"This time it is for always; so, as a parting souvenir, give to me the sweet English good-by."

As he said this, with a despairing sort of look, as if he could not spare even so humble a friend as myself, my heart was quite rent within me, and, regardless of several prim English ladies, I drew down his tall head and kissed him tenderly, feeling that in this world there were no more meetings for us. Then I ran away and buried myself in an empty railway carriage, hugging the little cologne bottle he had given me.

He promised to write, and for five years he has kept his word, sending me from Paris and Poland cheery, bright letters in English, at my desire, so that he might not forget. Here is one as a specimen.

MY DEAR AND GOOD FRIEND,

What do you think of me that I do not write so long time? Excuse me, my good mamma, for I was so busy in these days I could not do this pleasant thing. I write English without the fear that you laugh at it, because I know it is more agreeable to read the own language, and I think you are not excepted of this rule. It is good of me, for the expressions of love and regard, made with faults, take the funny appearance; they are *ridicule*, and instead to go to the heart, they make the laugh. Never mind, I do it.

You cannot imagine yourself how *stupide* is Paris when you are gone. I fly to my work, and make no more *fêtes* — it is too sad alone. I tie myself to my table and my *Vanity* (not of mine, for I am not vain, am I?). I wish some chapters to finish themselfs *vite*, that I send them to Pologne and know the end. I have a little question to ask you (of *Vanity* as always). I cannot translate this, no one of *dictionnaires* makes me the words, and I think it is *jargon de prison*, this little period. Behold:

> *"Mopy, is that your snum?"*
> *"Nubble your dad and gully the dog," &c.*

So funny things I cannot explain myself, so I send to you, and you reply sooner than without it, for you have so kind interest in my work you do not stay to wait. So this is a little hook for you to make you write some words to your son who likes it so much and is fond of you.

My doctor tells me my lungs are soon to be reestablished; so you may imagine yourself how glad I am, and of more courage in my future. You may one day see your Varjo in Amérique, if I study commerce as I wish. So then the last time of seeing ourselves is *not* the last. Is that to please you? I suppose the grand *histoire* is finished, *n'est-ce pas?* You will then send it to me care of M. Gryhomski Austriche, and he will give to me in clandestine way at Varsovie, otherwise it will be confiscated at the frontier by the *stupide* Russians.

Now we are dispersed in two sides of world far apart, for soon I go home to Pologne and am no more *juif errant*. It is now time I work at my life in some useful way, and I do it.

As I am your *grand fils*, it is proper that I make you my compliment of happy Christmas and New Year, is it not? I wish for you so many as they may fulfill long human life. May this year bring you more and more good hearts to love you (the only real happiness in the hard life), and may I be as now, yours for always,

VARJO

A year ago he sent me his photograph and a few lines. I acknowledged the receipt of it, but since then not a word has come, and I begin to fear that my boy is dead. Others have appeared to take his place, but they don't suit, and I keep his corner always ready for him if he lives. If he is dead, I am glad to have known so sweet and brave a character, for it does one good to see even as short-lived and obscure a hero as my Polish boy, whose dead December rose embalms for me the memory of Varjo, the last and dearest of my boys.

It is hardly necessary to add, for the satisfaction of inquisitive little women, that Laddie was the original of Laurie, as far as a pale pen and ink sketch could embody a living, loving boy.

In a later edition Miss Alcott has added to this account the fact of her seeing Ladislas Wisniewski some years after the former writing, and that he was by that time married and had come to America.